HIGHER-ORDER
Thinking
SKILLS

to Develop
21st Century
Learners

Author
Wendy Conklin, M.A.

Foreword
R. Bruce Williams

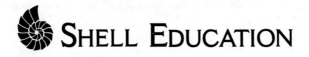

SHELL EDUCATION

Publishing Credits

Dona Herweck Rice, *Editor-in-Chief*; Robin Erickson, *Production Director*;
Lee Aucoin, *Creative Director*; Timothy J. Bradley, *Illustration Manager*;
Sara Johnson, M.S.Ed., *Senior Editor*; Evelyn Garcia, *Associate Education Editor*;
Juan Chavolla, *Cover/Interior Designer*; Corinne Burton, *M.A.Ed., Publisher*

Shell Education

5301 Oceanus Drive
Huntington Beach, CA 92649-1030
http://www.shelleducation.com
ISBN 978-1-4258-0822-8
©2012 Shell Educational Publishing, Inc.
WTP 3791

Table of Contents

Foreword

For those who have recognized the importance of teaching higher-order thinking skills, Wendy Conklin's book *Higher-Order Thinking Skills to Develop 21st Century Learners* will come as a welcome resource. Her summaries and documentation of those thinkers who have offered various approaches to thinking skills add the necessary depth to this book. Her inclusion of broad instructional models as well as specific classroom strategies brings the theory into practical application for the classroom.

Why bother with higher-order thinking skills? Tests (especially standardized tests) just ask for facts.

These days, more and more employment opportunities are requiring people who can think adroitly—and often think on their feet. In no way am I suggesting that learning facts is out of date. Rather, I am suggesting that facts and data alone will not cut it in our 21st century. This is not only because front-line workers are called upon to make critical judgments, but also because the data and information is constantly changing, evolving, and being updated. The task of evaluating new information is never-ending. For decades, we have heard the phrase "life-long learners." The necessity for this is truer than ever in this 21st century.

Relative to this question regarding the importance of higher-order thinking skills, be sure to read the section titled "The Necessity of Higher-Order Thinking Skills." In it, Conklin cites Stanley Pogrow's research using higher-order thinking skills with educationally disadvantaged students. The emphasis on these skills alone substantially increased the performance of those students in a variety of standardized tests. In addition, even standardized tests are moving to include material requiring facility in higher-order thinking skills.

In Chapter 2, Conklin analyzes the essential qualities of the 21st century thinker: asking questions, thinking strategically, using logical reasoning, exercising metacognition, and communicating effectively. While the 21st century thinker indeed needs to be familiar with facts, thinking needs to go beyond knowing the facts to being able to manipulate, evaluate, and apply them—all a part of the essential qualities of the 21st century thinker.

There are other materials on higher-order thinking skills. Why use this book?

This book is an up-to-date, comprehensive primer on the subject of higher-order thinking skills. As the title suggests, this is a book geared toward teaching and learning in the 21st century. For those who are intrigued with higher-order thinking skills but feel weak in the grasp of ongoing thinking in that field, Conklin gives important theoretical background. While making references to many of the higher-order thinking theoreticians of the previous century—such as John Dewey, Edward De Bono, Stanley Pogrow, and Richard Paul—Conklin goes into helpful detail with the updated model for Bloom's Taxonomy, Frank Williams' Taxonomy, and the Wallas Model.

For those who question when to begin working with students on these skills, Conklin provides a chapter on cognitive development. For those wondering what curriculum areas will be conducive to higher-order thinking skills, Conklin's chapter on platforms for higher-order thinking will be invaluable. For those wondering what various strategies and approaches will enhance these thinking skills, the extensive chapter on strategies will be exciting and motivating. Conklin even provides material on classroom management techniques, differentiation, and higher-order thinking skills for the English language learner. She concludes by addressing the questions of assessment and planning.

How can I learn one more complex model in addition to what I am already doing in the classroom?

It has long been my belief that emphasizing higher-order thinking skills is not so much a complex instructional model as it is the addition of a variety of simple strategies to enhance thinking. One simple strategy has to do with the kind of questions the teacher asks. It means asking more than yes-no questions. It means asking a question on how the student arrived at a response. It means asking students to wrestle with the material to compare and contrast or to explain why. It means asking students to figure out the relevance and meaning to his or her life. These questions do not take that much time, but end up dramatically transforming the classroom experience.

As Conklin emphasizes, the teacher can also enhance critical and creative thinking with graphic organizers, problem-solving exercises, decision-making strategies, games, creative activities, project-based learning, or very open-ended tasks.

Whether as a teacher you are adept at differentiation, cooperative learning, multiple intelligences, curriculum mapping, flexible grouping, or authentic assessment, you will easily increase the level of higher-order thinking skills in your classroom by incorporating material from this book into your teaching.

—R. Bruce Williams
Author of *Higher Order Thinking Skills:
Challenging All Students to Achieve*

Acknowledgements

My memory fails me when I think back to teachers offering me opportunities for higher-order thinking as a young student. But not too long ago, I stumbled upon a scrapbook filled with projects from my elementary school days. The humor in my India brochure surprised me. A teacher's note gave evidence of how I used my creative abilities to create a newscast as well as a slideshow to entertain parents at our open house. I pay tribute to those teachers who gave me open-ended assignments to complete so that my talents could shine. It was not until college that an American politics instructor forced me to think for myself as opposed to spouting out memorized facts. This instructor led me down the path to becoming a critical thinker—a priceless gift.

During my graduate years, I took a class on creativity taught by Sue Hodkinson, whose life was an inspiration to everyone who knew her. She taught me the value of pushing myself to be a more creative individual. That is the reason that as a 40-year-old, I enrolled in beginner guitar lessons. I am nowhere near being a competent guitarist yet, but taking lessons forces me to take risks and expand my abilities. Someday, I'll bring my guitar to professional development trainings. I have got a lot more practicing to do before then, though.

Now, as an adult, I am particularly aware of my children's creative and critical thinking, and I know to appreciate it. Dinnertimes are filled with lively conversation instigated by Jordan and Raegan. *If you could be any superhero, which one would you be and what powers would you have?* I make concerted efforts to teach them to think for themselves and to not believe everything they hear until they have checked out the facts. We discuss our biases as well as those of others. My children are the ones who make me utilize higher-order thinking daily.

I am grateful for many others who have had a role in my success in one way or another. For the kindergarten teachers at Chandler Oaks Elementary School, who so graciously granted me hours of their time in exchange for some measly pizza. For Sara Johnson, my wise editor who talks me back from the ledge when I get overwhelmed. For my husband, who supports my talents, even when it means tearing up our furniture for my latest reupholstering project or joining me at the gym for a challenging workout.

I am indebted to all of you for helping me see (in the words of Ralph Waldo Emerson) that it is not the length of life that I should covet, but the depth.

Thank you.

—Wendy Conklin

Chapter 1

A Brief Introduction to Higher-Order Thinking Skills

How in the world can I get my kids to think on higher levels when I have to worry about standardized tests?

Struggling students are not capable of higher-order thinking.

How do you teach higher-order thinking?

I've got too many English language learners in my class to worry about this right now.

It sounds like a waste of time. We've got to cover content!

I'm not creative myself, so how can I teach students to be that way?

Such are the comments, questions, or thoughts of many teachers. Today's educators are under a tremendous amount of pressure to enable students to successfully pass standardized tests, and many of their jobs depend on this. Some schools with struggling populations of students focus on just passing the test. Other schools with achieving populations concentrate their efforts on students receiving commendable scores on the tests. And while both of these are significant accomplishments and require a great deal of hard work, where does higher-order thinking fit into this context, and what makes it an important skill? To know the answer to this question, we first have to look closely at the characteristics of higher-order thinking, see what it has to do with rigor, and then examine how higher-order thinking benefits students.

Characteristics of Higher-Order Thinking Skills

Higher-order thinking skills encompass both critical thinking and creative thinking.

Critical thinking is the term that most people associate with higher-order thinking skills. It has been a buzzword in educational circles for some time. Everyone is in agreement when educational institutions say they want to produce students who are critical thinkers. Who does not want students to become critical thinkers? The topic is so popular that some colleges are even offering courses in critical thinking. So, what is critical thinking? Narrowly defined, critical thinking is characterized by careful analysis and judgment.

The National Council for Excellence in Critical Thinking Instruction says, "Critical thinking is self-guided, self-disciplined thinking which attempts to reason at the highest level of quality in a fair-minded way. People who think critically consistently attempt to live rationally, reasonably, empathically" (Scriven and Paul 1987). What Scriven and Paul are saying is that when critical thinkers are posed with a problem, they prompt their learning. They commit themselves to think logically about a topic and refuse to jump to conclusions. They struggle to put away the biases that come so naturally and endeavor to look at a situation in a new way so that it can be analyzed and evaluated in a logical manner. And, they reflect on what they learned.

John Dewey was a believer in reflective thinking. He described reflective thinking as an active, persistent, and careful review of something that is believed (Dewey 1916). The active learner does not just accept information passively. He or she looks for evidence to support the information. If no evidence is found, the piece of information cannot be believed. Instead of being told what to think, a person must think for himself or herself. And he or she must give good cause for the conclusions that are reached. In essence, reflective thinking is critical thinking. It is thinking about thinking, what some people refer to as metacognition. It is taking control of learning and being continually conscious and committed to asking *why*. A more contemporary expert in the field has said it this way: "Critical thinking is reasonable, reflective thinking that is focused on deciding what to believe or do" (Norris and Ennis 1989).

Creative thinking is also a higher-order thinking skill and is equally as important as critical thinking. In the book *Curriculum 21: Essential Education for a Changing World*, Heidi Hayes Jacobs says that curriculum should go beyond giving tools for reasonable and logical thinking. Curriculum should also nurture creativity in all learners (Jacobs 2010).

Inventing and synthesizing characterizes creative thinking. *Create* means to bring something into existence that was not there previously. And, that which was brought into existence must have value. Creative thinking is the process of bringing about a new idea.

Lest anyone misunderstand, creative thinking is work. Like critical thinking, creative thinking is also active. Michael Michalko, author of *Thinkertoys: A Handbook of Creative-Thinking Techniques*, says, "Creativity is not an accident, not something that is genetically determined. It is not a result of some easily learned magic trick or secret, but a consequence of your intention to be creative and your determination to learn and use creative-thinking strategies" (2006, Introduction XVII).

As noted previously, many people erroneously believe that some are born with creativity and some are not. A leading authority in the field of creative thinking, Edward De Bono, says creativity is a skill that everyone can learn and have (2008). He says that not everyone will have the same outcomes or skill levels. Just as some people are better at playing basketball, some people will be better at creativity than others. However, all people can learn how to play basketball, and all people can learn the skill of creative thinking.

While we are on the topic of creativity, let us talk about being creative teachers. I work with many teachers in workshops around the country who insist that they are not creative individuals. I believe they are wrong. Negativity keeps teachers from being creative. They do not believe they can be creative. In believing these things, teachers have let their attitudes determine their abilities. Michalko says, "Every time we pretend to have an attitude and go through the motions, we trigger the emotions we create and strengthen the attitude we wish to cultivate…To be creative, you have to believe and act as if you are creative…Once you believe you are creative, you will begin to believe in the worth of your ideas, and you will have the persistence to implement them" (2006, Introduction XIV). Regardless of what teachers' abilities really are, to be the very best teachers (the kind of teachers who change students' lives), they must be creative

How can teachers plan higher-order thinking lessons? The idea is to start small, with just one lesson a week. They can enlist the help of other teachers, use the strategies in this book, and search for activities that promote higher-order thinking. Teachers can have the insight to see opportunities when students pose good questions and know what to do in those situations. Being creative is essential to being a good teacher. These teachers will appreciate creativity when they see it in their students, knowing that this behavior will benefit their students.

Both critical-thinking skills and creative-thinking skills come together under the heading of higher-order thinking skills that are grounded in lower-level thinking. To think about a topic at a higher level, understanding that topic is a given. Students have to know the basic facts, understand the concepts, and apply what they know so that they can pick the topic apart through analysis, make a judgment call, or create something new based on the idea. For example, when students are asked to create a new setting of a story and then tell how that would change the story, students must know the definition of a setting in a story. The more complex question is built upon the basic question. Another example would be asking students to write an adventure story about visiting a planet in the solar system, using actual facts about the planet. Students incorporate all the facts they learn, but also produce a product that is original and creative. Again, higher-order thinking in this example is based on understanding lower-level facts.

Is Bloom's Taxonomy Related to Higher-Order Thinking?

Most teachers are familiar with Bloom's Taxonomy of the Cognitive Domain, more commonly called Bloom's Taxonomy. In a nutshell, Bloom's Taxonomy classifies intellectual behavior into six levels of thinking. The lowest levels of thinking require basic recognition or recall. The highest levels of thinking require critical and creative thinking. (In recent years, Bloom's Taxonomy has undergone a makeover of sorts. The reasons for this will be addressed more thoroughly in Chapter 5.) Categorizing higher-order thinking skills in this way often makes sense for many teachers because it is something with which they are familiar. For years, it has been part of undergraduate teacher-preparatory classes and professional development for current teachers. Bloom's Taxonomy has a significant role in helping us understand higher-order thinking skills.

Rigor Is Involved

According to Strong, Silver, and Perini, "rigor is the goal of helping students develop the capacity to understand content that is complex, ambiguous, provocative, and personally or emotionally challenging" (2001, 7).

Think about the types of content that are listed above in this definition. If we take this definition apart, we see that rigor has many facets. Some content is more complex than others, which makes it more rigorous. For example, the recession that many countries around the world experienced during 2010 would be a rigorous topic to study because it is comprised of many layers of complexity. Content that is ambiguous does not offer just one problem or one answer—it offers multiple things to sort and consider. Provocative content is rigorous because it conceptually challenges students to face dilemmas, identify problems, engage in inquiry, and take sides in arguments, such as W. E. B. Du Bois and Booker T. Washington's diverse approaches to equality for African Americans. Rigorous content that challenges students emotionally or personally could be displayed by covering topics in the Middle East, or abolitionist John Brown's actions at Harper's Ferry.

In their book, *Teaching What Matters Most: Standards and Strategies for Raising Student Achievement*, the authors state strongly that *all* students need rigorous content. They assert the belief that one of the reasons that schools fail is that they withhold rigor from some of their students. They feel that all students, regardless of ability levels, need rigorous content with whatever direct instruction is needed to manage the complex content (Strong, Silver, and Perini 2001).

So how does rigor fit in with higher-order thinking skills? Rigorous content provides students a venue through which they can use higher-level thinking skills. Rigor cannot be accomplished if it is not coupled with thinking skills.

All standards are written with some level of thinking or cognition required by the student. For example, the student will understand that the universe is made up of planets. This standard requires a very low level of rigor and low level of thinking. The student will analyze the planets to find which ones have a more conducive environment for life. This standard requires a higher level of rigor and a higher level of thinking. Rigor stresses *quality* over *quantity*. Rigor and higher-order thinking go hand in hand. Students incorporate higher-order thinking when they encounter rigorous content. It is a happy marriage. You cannot have one without the other.

The Necessity of Higher-Order Thinking Skills

While it sounds good to say that never has there been a more urgent time when we need to encourage our students to develop and use higher-order thinking skills, there has never been a time in history when this was *not* needed. And, it is still as important as it has ever been for *at least* two very simple reasons: we want our students to be successful in school, and we want them to grow up to be adults who contribute positively to society.

Do higher-order thinking skills contribute to academic achievement? Stanley Pogrow (2005) is the creator of a curriculum called HOTS which emphasizes higher-order thinking skills. More than 25 years ago, he started his program for educationally disadvantaged students. These students either had learning disabilities or were identified for the Title I program. The goal of HOTS was to increase test scores and academic achievement by increasing socialization skills and thinking skills. No extra test drills or teaching to the test were included. Over time, 2,600 schools with about half a million disadvantaged students adopted his program. These schools used a variety of standardized tests so that the program could not be tailored to any one certain test. Subsequent results have shown that these economically disadvantaged students' scores significantly increased in both reading comprehension and mathematics.

When considering the necessity of higher-order thinking skills, it is important to think about what happens to students when they leave the classrooms. Students eventually grow into adults. These adults make decisions that, at times, affect all of us globally. At other times, these adults' decisions affect those immediately around them. No one lives in a vacuum. Teaching students how to think both critically and creatively is a priceless gift. It will affect how they live the rest of their lives and will make them lifelong learners.

When students watch commercials on television, many of them believe everything that is said. But, they are not the only ones who get taken in by these commercials. Many adults fall for this, too. It is in our nature, as people, to be passive. It is so much easier to be a passive receiver of this information than it is to be an active receiver. My own kids hear a rumor on the Internet about their favorite movie star, and they assume that it is true. No higher-order thinking is involved. And they continue believing the rumor until I ask them how they know that this rumor is true. They pause and think about it. They try to support their views and look for other proof. Suddenly, they are active learners instead of passive learners.

Many classrooms center on creating passive receivers of information. Who of us is not guilty of telling our students what to think instead of how to think for themselves? It is in teachers' nature to enjoy being important, or at least important enough to tell our students what to think. Students have to listen to their teachers, or at least pretend to listen. Perhaps that is why some students complain of boring classes. Higher-order thinking causes students to struggle and requires that students be active learners. Active learning is hard work, but it is also fun and engaging.

How does a teacher set up a classroom that transforms passive thinkers into active thinkers? The first step to doing this is for teachers to stop being the provider of all information. This does not mean that teachers stop teaching or planning what needs to be taught. On the contrary, it means that teachers begin crafting lessons that demand more from students than just recalling, summarizing, and identifying. But, how do we do that? Specific strategies that can be infused in content will be discussed in detail in Chapter 5.

In recent years, it seems that some teachers have gotten away from the idea that learning is fun. Teachers need to remember that there is excitement and satisfaction in learning. As an adult, I love grappling with something that is ambiguous or controversial. I have found the joy of facing my own biases and seeking to either change them or validate them with proof. This process of higher-order thinking makes us come alive. It makes us care. And I would argue that it makes us better human beings. Teaching lessons that are infused with higher-order thinking skills will make the classroom come alive, too. Students will awaken and care about the content and, in the process, reach the ultimate goal of learning.

Conclusion

Higher-order thinking skills encompass both critical and creative thinking. This requires learners to be active, not passive. A student is an active learner when he or she analyzes, evaluates, and creates. When a student is a receiver of information, he or she is a passive learner. Concrete examples of higher-order thinking can be easily seen in the top three levels of Bloom's Taxonomy of the Cognitive Domain. Rigor and higher-order thinking go hand-in-hand because students naturally use higher-order thinking when they encounter rigorous content. The benefits of infusing higher-order thinking skills in the classroom are twofold. Higher-order thinking skills will increase academic achievement as well as produce lifelong learners.

Let's Think and Discuss

1. In what ways have you used higher-order thinking skills in your classroom?

2. When studying about any subject, is it a necessity that students think on lower levels first before they can successfully use higher-order thinking? Why or why not?

3. How do you feel your students will respond to using higher-order thinking skills?

Chapter 2

The 21st Century Thinker

Essential Qualities of a 21st Century Thinker

Many schools around the world are focusing their attention on producing 21st century thinkers. These thinkers are defined by what they can do in this ever-changing world. Undoubtedly, the world has changed tremendously in the past 100 years. And, the world continues to change at a rapid pace, thanks to technology.

To be sure school curriculum prepares students adequately, various organizations have put together models and frameworks that explain the common themes and concepts that promote thinking skills and will help students compete successfully in the 21st century.

The Partnership for 21st Century Skills (2004) is an organization based in the United States that "advocates for 21st century readiness for every student." Its framework defines what students need to succeed in both work and life during the 21st century.

The International Society for Technology in Education, or ISTE, has identified the following six educational technology standards for students that promote 21st century skills (2007):

- Creativity and innovation—Students **demonstrate** creative thinking, **construct** knowledge, and **develop** innovative products and processes using technology.

- Communication and collaboration—Students use digital media and environments to **communicate** and work collaboratively, including communicating at a distance, to support individual learning and **contribute** to the learning of others.

- Research and informational fluency—Students will apply digital tools to **gather**, **evaluate**, and **use** information.

- Critical thinking, problem solving, and decision making—Students use critical-thinking skills to **plan** and **conduct** research, **manage** projects, **solve** problems, and **make** informed decisions, using appropriate digital tools and resources.

- Digital citizenship—Students **understand** human, cultural, and societal issues related to technology and **practice** legal and ethical behavior.

- Technology operations and concepts—Students **demonstrate** a sound understanding of technological concepts, systems, and operations.

All these frameworks, models, and curricula are the means to an end. The result is to produce 21st century thinkers. How will we know when we have arrived there? 21st century thinkers exhibit the following qualities:

- Willingness to ask questions

- Strategic thinking skills

- Logical reasoning

- Knowledge of how to exercise metacognition

- Ability to make inferences

- Ability to problem-solve

- Innovation and creativity

- Emotional intelligence

- Effective communication skills

21st Century Thinkers Ask Questions

What if classrooms focused on getting students to *ask* questions instead of *answer* questions? This type of classroom is desirable because it transforms a somewhat passive classroom into an active learning environment. The teacher can transform the classroom into one that is conducive to getting students to ask questions. However, the atmosphere of a classroom must be twofold in this respect: Students must be comfortable asking questions, and the teacher must be comfortable with not knowing all the answers.

Getting students to ask the questions can be a tough task. It has to begin by modeling this for the students. Begin by asking thought-provoking questions. Ask questions aloud that cannot be answered. This modeling will go a long way in teaching students how to ask questions. Talk about the difference between "fat questions" and "skinny questions." Fat questions can have more than one answer, if any answer at all, whereas skinny questions are shallow and do not require much thought. They are easy to answer and do not challenge us to use higher-order thinking skills. Probe the students' thinking. Be the devil's advocate.

Is asking questions of the students a bad thing? No, not at all. Obviously, many questions are derived from the fact that teachers need to assess students' knowledge. How can teachers know where to begin if they do not know where students need them to begin? Teachers do this by asking questions, which is both good and valid. However, is it possible to assess students by the questions that they ask? Yes. One way to do this is to have students write down their questions for you to grade. For example, instead of having students write down all they know about a topic, have them write questions they have about the topic. This can tell teachers what students know and do not know. Or, students can verbalize their questions. Teachers can set up an audio recording and have students read their questions into the recorder. This is perfect for English language learners because some of their writing skills are not as developed. It also takes away the factor of embarrassment and stress if they happen to say their question in front of the class with errors.

The second part of this task is being comfortable with not having answers for your students. It takes a transparent teacher to admit that he or she does not know everything. I frequently conduct professional development on using primary sources in the classroom. As I do, I have many candid conversations with teachers during the professional development. We frequently discuss how to handle situations when the teacher does not know the answer to a question. This can be very stressful for teachers. I tell them it is all right to not know the answers. In fact, it is virtually impossible to always know the answers. During the years I spent teaching, I taught many gifted students. The older they were, the more intimidating they became. However, I had a 7-year-old who joined an online class about amusement park physics that was geared for 10- to 12-year-olds. While physics is not my forte, I did take this course in high school. I understood the basics of Newton's laws of motion and understood how they applied to amusement park rides in a simplistic way. But this 7-year-old made me learn physics in panic mode. I spent hours preparing for our online discussions each week because I knew he would ask some tough questions, mostly ones that I could not answer. He had a way of explaining the laws of motion by using very practical everyday examples so that my other students (and I) understood it better. I had to psych myself up and convince myself that it was all right that this student was "smarter" than I was about this topic. This student challenged me to be a learner. As teachers, being vulnerable will help students feel comfortable asking their questions. When in this situation, teachers can respond with, "I do not know the answer, but we can try to find out."

21st Century Thinkers Think Strategically

What does it mean to think strategically? Strategic thinking is deliberate thinking, and is sometimes referred to as 'clever thinking.' The decisions that are made are based on a desired outcome, and determine that outcome. It is a way of identifying goals and then working backward to make those goals come to fruition. It involves long-term goal setting and then making daily decisions based on those goals as well as global decisions based on those goals. Think of the game of chess. Every move a player makes affects the outcome in one way or another. Skilled players make deliberate moves and hope to outsmart their opponents. Strategic thinking is not just for game playing, though. It is an important skill for life. Strategic-thinking adults make decisions about investments with a goal in mind. They take deliberate steps and are goal-oriented. Below are some generic steps to thinking strategically.

1. Strategic thinkers first think about where they want to be. What is the goal?

2. They ask how they will know when they reach that goal. They look for some type of feedback.

3. They look at where they are right now. What are the problems they face?

4. They think about ways to get to their goals. What steps do they need to take?

5. Strategic thinkers look at the future. What ongoing things will they have to address to continue down their path toward the desired outcome?

Practicing strategic thinking helps students develop those decision-making skills that prepare them for adulthood. When they have to clean up their dirty room so they can go to a friend's house, they make strategic decisions on what to clean first. Do they pick up all the clothes and then pick up the toys? Do they just clean what they run into as they make their way through their room? This takes some strategic thinking so they can get to the goal of playing at a friend's house. The more something is practiced, the more likely it will be used. Students use strategic thinking in small ways when they solve difficult mathematical problems. Teachers can set up scenarios like an "Economics Day," when students have to launch a business and sell a product or service.

21st Century Thinkers Use Logical Reasoning

The process of reasoning allows teachers to go beyond the given information. We use logical reasoning to clarify problems and figure out solutions. Logical reasoning uses both deductive and inductive thinking to solve problems.

Deductive thinking is characterized by elimination. It is the "if this, then that" type of thinking. A person might be given some clues and then must use those clues to come to a logical conclusion. For example, think of a mystery movie you have watched lately. There were clues given all along the way to help you solve it. Logic puzzlers are used by some teachers to help students practice deductive thinking.

For example, *if A = B and B = C, then A = C.*

Or, *Sara has one brother but three sisters-in-law. How is this possible?*

Another example would include the following puzzler: *There are three pizzas: cheese, pepperoni, and supreme. José likes all kinds of meat pizzas. Anna is a vegetarian. Mark only likes one topping on his pizza. Decide who ate each of the pizzas.*

Deductive thinking is narrow and challenges us to test our hypothesis to find an answer. It feels natural to us, we practice this all the time.

Inductive thinking provides the answer, but one must work backward to make sense of the answer. It moves from specific observations to broader generalizations and understanding. You look for patterns along the way to make sense of the conclusion. This is a clever way of creating movies, writing books, or showing a television show. One of my favorite movies is *Memento* (2000). In the film, the main character suffers from short-term memory loss, so he tattoos his body with clues to help him remember key pieces of information and find out who murdered his wife. The movie begins with the last scene, and part of the movie is told in reverse-chronological order. Viewers must piece together the clues to help them make sense of the final conclusion, which they already know. *Time's Arrow* (1991) by Martin Amis deals with the events of the Holocaust by traveling backwards in time. "Seinfeld" fans might recall one of the final episodes called "The Betrayal" (1997), in which the events are shown in reverse chronological order beginning with Jerry, Elaine, and George returning from a disastrous trip to India. Inductive thinking challenges us to explore so that we can come to a general theory or understanding.

21st Century Thinkers Exercise Metacognition

Thinking involves the operation of cognition. Cognition is the capacity to acquire knowledge through reasoning. Everyone has some degree of cognitive ability. Some of us are better thinkers than others. And, there are some people who take the next step and think about their thinking processes. They are able to step outside themselves and look at how they think. They are conscious of their thinking. And, they problem solve as they think. This is called *metacognition*.

Metacognition is often referred to as *thinking about thinking*. This can be broadly characterized by planning before acting. The entire course of action is planned, and then the task is begun. Throughout the task, people monitor themselves and make adjustments where necessary. Finally, when the task is complete, they evaluate the end result. Metacognition requires deliberate actions.

Think about what this type of thinking would do to our lives if we implemented it all the time. Then think about how this would enhance students' ability to learn in the classroom. It is important for students to be aware of how they think and how others think. This awareness helps us to develop our thinking skills further, and it also increases our confidence as thinkers. For example, Rashona, a fifth-grade student, wants to explain what led to her course of action, and so it makes Rashona think about her thinking and it shows others in the class how she thinks. They can add Rashona's strategy to their toolkit for solving future problems. Problems will not seem as intimidating if students know that there are tools they can use to arrive at viable solutions.

In the book *Developing a Thinking Skills Program* (1988), Beyer says that metacognition guides, manages, and drives the use of thinking skills. According to Beyer, metacognitive strategies include planning, monitoring, and assessing. The skills are presented in the table below.

Strategies	Skills
Planning	• Stating a goal • Selecting operations to perform • Sequencing operations • Identifying potential obstacles/errors • Identifying ways to recover from obstacles/errors • Predicting results desired and/or anticipated
Monitoring	• Keeping the goal in mind • Keeping one's place in a sequence • Knowing when a subgoal has been achieved • Deciding when to go on to the next operation • Selecting the next appropriate operation • Spotting errors or obstacles • Knowing how to recover from errors, overcome obstacles
Assessing	• Assessing goal achievement • Judging accuracy and adequacy of the results • Evaluating appropriateness of procedures used • Assessing and handling of obstacles/errors • Judging efficiency of the plan and its execution

(Beyer 1988)

There are specific things teachers can do to encourage metacognition. Teachers can prompt discussions in class about how students problem-solve. For example, how did they solve a mathematics problem? Let students share their strategies. Then compare how students approached and solved the problem.

Second, teachers can have students analyze their learning styles to think about how they learn best. Do they enjoy group work, or do they prefer to work individually? Do they prefer games or projects? What makes them tick?

Third, teachers can challenge students to explain where their viewpoints came from. How did they make their decisions to do something? While it is good for students to argue their cases, it is also important for them to examine their thinking. To help with this, assign students the task of defending the opposing viewpoints (Barell 1984, 1991a, 1991b). For example, defending Galileo's viewpoint that Earth is not the center of the universe is easy to do today because of advancements in technology. Instead, take the Church's viewpoint and defend it. This helps students to understand what happened and why.

Asking students to explain the reasons for their actions prompts this kind of thinking. For example, I have discovered that when my work does not demand enough creativity from me, I begin redecorating my house—repainting rooms, upholstering furniture, and rearranging so that I can get my "creativity fix." I have spent time thinking about why I do what I do because I have an exasperated family who wonders why our home is occasionally in a messy upheaval. I am now aware of my actions, but not before I was challenged to think about the reasons why I make those choices.

Teachers can model how students can understand what they know, what else they need to know, and finally how to get that knowledge. Teachers can also point out directly when something has involved critical thinking or why something is creative. Students can practice metacognition by keeping daily journals, writing summaries, listing expectations, and completing self-evaluations (Leader 1995).

21st Century Thinkers Make Inferences

An inference is a conclusion drawn from evidence or reasoning. It is more than just a stab in the dark or making a guess about something. Logical reasoning and evidence are necessary to support inferences. Depending on the content, the term *inference* can take on varied but similar meanings.

Making inferences is a widely discussed topic in regards to reading comprehension. It is reading between the lines to make meaning. The process of inferring involves making connections, identifying main ideas and details, struggling with questions, understanding point of view and bias, and developing theories, conclusions, and evaluations about the information (Macceca 2007; Keene and Zimmermann 1997).

An inference in science is drawing conclusions based on information that is already known from a sampling of data. It is not just a guess or stab in the dark; rather, it is an educated guess. It can be a hypothesis or theory of how something works and that needs to be tested. Or, it can be the result of a test or experiment. As new evidence is found, inferences change. A sufficient amount of data can help solidify the accuracy of an inference.

In mathematics, an inference is usually associated with rules. Inference making is the process of using deductive thinking to come to a conclusion.

Students who are 21st century thinkers employ inferences as they reason through topics to find ultimate conclusions or answers.

21st Century Thinkers Can Problem-Solve

There is one thing that teachers can know for sure: There will always be problems to solve. Successful problem solvers do two things really well. They first define or clarify the problem. Then, they search for solutions to the problem.

First, let us look at how teachers can help students define or clarify problems. At times, the real problem can be difficult to identify. It might need to be simplified so that it can be understood. A teacher can be instrumental in helping students focus and pinpoint the real problem by probing with questions or by modeling it for them. According to Davis and Rimm (1998), the following exercises can be helpful when trying to define problems:

- Isolate the important aspects of a problem—What is relevant? What is essential? What should we focus on? What can we ignore?

- Identify the subproblems—What problems are related to the main problem? What problems will follow from each solution?

- Define the problems more broadly—This might help open up new solution possibilities.

Next, let us look at how a teacher can help his or her students search for solutions to problems. This can involve strategies already discussed in this chapter. Learning how to strategically think and to logically think are two strategies that can be taught to students. Teachers can show students how to brainstorm effectively by modeling this technique in class. For example, students can be placed in groups where they work together on a project relevant to the topic of study. This experience can teach students to appreciate the various strengths that classmates possess. Students will learn to be better problem solvers as they practice solving problems together. As teachers model how to problem-solve, students will be able to use the strategies learned to solve problems on their own. As always, students should share how they problem-solve to encourage metacognition and so that others can learn from their thinking.

21st Century Thinkers Innovate and Create

Remember, the definition for the framework for 21st century learning included creativity and innovation skills. If we think about what the future might hold, we can see how we need people who can demonstrate originality and inventiveness in their work. We need people who can develop, implement, and communicate new ideas to others. We need those who are open and responsive to diverse perspectives and can act on creative ideas to make tangible and useful contributions to the domain in which the innovation occurs.

Creativity is important and should be part of learning in our classrooms. Remember, cultivating a culture of creativity is just as important as critical thinking (Jacobs 2010). There are strategies that can be interwoven into curriculum to provide students the opportunity to practice being creative. Here are some ways that teachers can do this:

- Ask questions that do not have only one answer.

- Show verbal appreciation for students who do not always do the "normal things" or give the typical or expected answers. This creative thinking strategy is good for our classrooms, and it is good for our society.

21st Century Thinkers Possess Emotional Intelligence

Peter Salovey and John Mayer (1990) use the term *emotional intelligence* to explain how certain people understand their own feelings and have empathy for one another's feelings. They say it is "the regulation of emotion in a way that enhances living" (1990, 267). Salovey and Mayer proposed that emotional intelligence consisted of five characteristics:

- **Self-awareness**—recognizing feelings when they occur

- **Self-regulation**—the ability to manage emotions and impulses

- **Motivation**—having a goal to reach

- **Empathy**—recognizing emotion in others

- **Social skills**—handling relationships

Recently, Daniel Goleman (2006) has popularized emotional intelligence in his book of the same title. He states that emotional intelligence is a set of skills that can include control of one's impulses, self-motivation, empathy, and social competence when dealing with interpersonal relationships. He believes that emotional intelligence is more important than intelligence that is measured by regular IQ tests when measuring a person's success.

How does emotional intelligence help us? Self-aware people have coping mechanisms in place. A test developed by Harvard psychologist Robert Rosenthal measures how sensitive people are to nonverbal clues. The test found that children with high scores did better in school and were more popular than those who did not score well. It did not matter that many of these high scorers on the EQ test had only mediocre IQ test scores (Gibbs 1995). This implies that students who have strong people skills (empathy, social skills, and graciousness) tend to be more successful adults than those who do not.

Practically speaking, schools have encouraged emotional intelligence by offering courses in conflict resolution, social skills, anger management, and impulse control.

21st Century Thinkers Communicate Effectively

Many leaders we admire most from history were great communicators. They understood the public, and the public understood them. To communicate effectively, one must transmit feelings so as to be understood clearly.

Communication is more than just talking. Today, technology has made communication around the world as easy as the click of a button. We can videoconference, email, and blog—all of which are ways to communicate our ideas with others. We are becoming a global society, so these particular communication skills are important ones for the 21st century.

We can have all the creativity and critical-thinking skills that exist, but if we cannot communicate what we know, then what good are those skills? Most people are not born with strong communication skills; for most of us, these skills are learned.

Teachers spend much of their time helping students clarify their thoughts with written responses. They require that students write papers, defend opinions, and explain their thoughts. All this practice can successfully help students to understand how to communicate effectively, so keep on doing it! To these writing standards, add in the skills that transfer to technology. Students today need to be taught how to comment *appropriately* on blogs. They need to understand the limits of social networking and what should and *should not* be shared. Emails can easily be interpreted as void of emotion, so students must take extra strides to communicate with emotion so that their words can be understood. Model what a good blog post looks like as well as an ineffective blog post. By doing what we have done well for so long, and also including new ways of communicating (thanks to technology), we can help our students to be well-rounded and effective 21st century thinkers.

Conclusion

Twenty-first century thinkers are the inquisitive ones who ask the questions. They think strategically, with goals in mind. They know how to incorporate logical reasoning when solving problems. They think about their thinking (metacognition) and know the whys behind their actions. They naturally make inferences and are not afraid of problem solving because they know what strategies and skills to use to get the job done. These thinkers are innovators and creators. They possess emotional intelligence and know themselves and others well by picking up on social cues. And finally, 21st century thinkers put great effort into communicating effectively.

Let's Think and Discuss

1. In what ways are you a 21st century thinker?

2. As a teacher, how do you learn best? This might shed some light on your teaching style and open your mind to teaching in new ways.

3. What is one practical thing you can do to help students reach the goal of being a 21st century thinker?

Chapter 3

Cognitive Development and Higher-Order Thinking

Young children are not capable of using higher-order thinking skills.

Why don't you just lay off and let them be children?

You need to wait until students understand the basics before teaching higher-order thinking.

Starting in fifth grade, students can practice higher-order thinking.

When Can Students Think Critically?

How old do you need to be to use higher-order thinking skills?

Jean Piaget (1969) is the psychologist best known for his theory of cognitive development. He believed that children could not learn something until their intellectual capabilities were mature enough. Their ability to learn is directly related to their stage of intellectual development. Piaget's theory impacts curriculum and instruction in the sense that both must be developmentally appropriate for children and take into account how cognitive structures are formed. Piaget's four stages are shown in the table below.

Piaget's Cognitive-Development Theory

Stage	Age	Abilities
sensorimotor	birth–2 years old	The child interacts physically with his or her environment and builds the concept of reality.
preoperational	3–7 years old	The child cannot think abstractly yet and needs concrete situations.
concrete operations	8–11 years old	Children begin to form concepts out of observations, experience, and data, and are capable of thinking abstractly.
formal operations	12–15 years old	Children begin to think similarly to adults and can think abstractly with reasoning abilities.

Piaget's theory can impact the use of higher-order thinking skills in the classroom. Does Piaget's theory also mean that we cannot expect students younger than 12 to think both critically and creatively? Once a student turns 12, do we just expect him or her to begin thinking critically? Common sense tells teachers "no" to both of these questions. And trying to cite Piaget's work to say that young children cannot think critically is a misuse of the research, in my opinion.

The Impact of the Classroom on Brain Growth

What happens in the classroom can have a large impact on brain growth. Eric Jensen (1998) argues that classroom environment, enrichment/challenge, and feedback are key to brain growth, and says that the classroom environment should provide enrichment for *all* students.

Jensen bases his belief of classroom environment on research conducted by Frederick Goodwin, the former director of the Institute of Mental Health. Likewise, Kotulak's work shows that a person's IQ can change based on the learning environment. In fact, it can increase or decrease by 20 points (Kotulak 1996). For example, if a classroom is a negative experience for a student who has a 110 IQ, this student's IQ could drop to as low as 90. A negative classroom is characterized by sarcasm, embarrassment, humiliation, finger pointing, and unrealistic deadlines. On the other hand, if the classroom is a positive and stimulating environment, the student's IQ could jump to 130. A positive classroom is characterized by encouragement, camaraderie, challenge, and feedback (Jensen 1998).

Enrichment and challenge are also important for brain growth. Neuroscientist Bob Jacobs and colleagues (Jacobs, Schall, Scheibel 1993) conducted research on graduate students and found that the students who experienced challenging activities showed more than 25 percent in brain growth compared to graduate students who just coasted through their classes without challenge. These studies tell us that students need challenging activities to encourage brain growth.

The amount of challenge that is presented is key for brain growth. University of Chicago professor Mihaly Csikszentmihalyi describes a concept called *flow*. Flow is "being completely involved in an activity for its own sake. The ego falls away. Time flies. Every action, movement, and thought follows inevitably from the previous one, like playing jazz. Your whole being is involved, and you're using your skills to the utmost" (quoted in Geirland 1996). This idea of *flow* is helpful to understanding how to challenge students appropriately in the classroom. Figure 3.1 on the following page shows that the right amount of challenge based on students' skills will create a learning flow that engages students without overwhelming or boring them. Too much challenge produces anxiety, too little produces boredom.

Fig. 3.1 Example of a learning flow

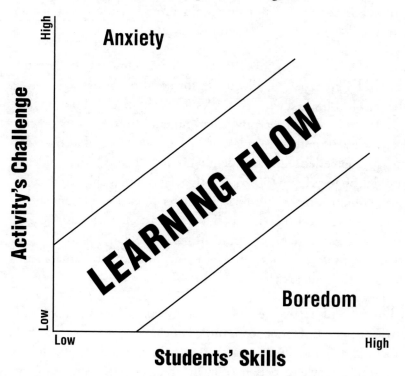

Finally, feedback is necessary for brain growth and is most useful when it is immediate feedback. The brain operates on feedback (Harth 1995). Students need feedback to reduce the stress and uncertainty. When stress is reduced, brain growth increases. Are they doing a good job? Are they on track? Are they progressing? Teachers can provide feedback by giving verbal acknowledgement, written comments, peer evaluations, cooperative learning, and conferencing, just to name a few.

Using Higher-Order Thinking to Challenge Students

Teachers can challenge students by using higher-order thinking skills. These skills need to be taught within content, must be centered on something meaningful, and should be developmentally appropriate.

Research shows that thinking skills should be taught within content and not in isolation (Carr 1988; Rowland-Dunn 1989; Smith 1990). "Teaching thinking operations in subject-matter courses not only enhances learning to these operations but also contributes to increased achievement in subject-matter learning" (Beyer 1987, 8). In other words, teachers need to infuse the content of each lesson with opportunities for students to think both critically and creatively so that they will learn. This can be accomplished in the kinds of questions that are asked, the types of activities available to students, and the products students create.

Higher-order thinking should be done in context of something meaningful and relevant. Sue Bredekamp says, "Learning information in meaningful context is not only essential for children's understanding and development of concepts, but is also important for stimulating motivation in children. If learning is relevant for children, they are more likely to persist with a task and to be motivated to learn more" (1990, 51–53). When a teacher begins asking higher-order questions, it needs to be done with topics and content that are familiar to students. In other words, it must be about something they understand. These questions should also be based on something that is interesting to students. Students must care about it to bother thinking about it. Making the conversations both familiar and interesting provides a safe environment. Students will feel that they can answer questions based on what they know about. It is concrete. Then, teachers can apply the higher-order questions to something that is standards-based.

A teacher of young students must marry the use of higher-order thinking with developmentally appropriate activities. For example, no one would expect a kindergartner to be able to understand the consequences of European exploration on the American Indians at the same level as a sixth grader would. But even young students can learn to solve problems, brainstorm ideas, analyze images, express their opinions, and compare and contrast two concrete objects within subject matter that is developmentally appropriate.

Reasons to Begin Early

It is important for students in early elementary school to utilize higher-order thinking for brain growth. According to Jensen, "the brain learns fastest and easiest during the early school years." In fact, simple, concrete problem solving can begin at age 1 or 2 (1998, 32). Brain growth increases as students are given complex, challenging problems to solve. Exposing students to a variety of ways to solve problems is also crucial to brain growth (Gardner 1993). Jensen (1998) says that the brain's growth is not dependent on discovering the right *solution* to the problem. Instead, it is the problem-solving *process* that increases brain growth. And, opportunities like this cannot begin too early in school: "it makes sense to encourage youngsters to do any problem-solving activity; the more real life, the better" (1998, 36). Additionally, Jensen states that experiences like science experiments and building projects are beneficial for very young students.

Another reason to use higher-order thinking with young students early on is to begin the development of these skills. "The early developing brain grows the fastest and is the most ready for change" (Jensen 1998, 40). The opportunities to grow young brains by starting early must be seized. If students reach fifth grade and have never had to think for themselves, it will be tough getting these students to do it. It will take a major shift in how these learners think and act. Why not start early and develop the skills right away so that when students are 12 years old, they are more fluently using higher-order thinking?

How to Develop Higher-Order Thinking Early

Kindergarten can be one of the best places for critical and creative thinking, says Kendall Ganong, a kindergarten teacher in the Round Rock Independent School District in Texas. "At this age, they are curious about everything. They ask questions and want to know about anything and everything. I think it is more how we, as teachers, guide the conversations and discussions that take place. It is better if they are the inquirers, and we guide them on how to figure it all out."

I spent some time in Ganong's classroom, observing her introduction to a unit about bats. Her questions—and more importantly, her students' questions—showed that they were inquirers. I decided that the best place to understand how to encourage higher-order thinking is by observing these kindergarten students and by interviewing their teachers. I met with the kindergarten teachers at Ganong's school. The following shows the progression of our discussion on the topic of higher-order thinking.

1. How do you help your students develop higher-order thinking (critical thinking and creative thinking) skills?

   Teachers need to encourage questions. It is natural for kindergarten students to ask questions. And when students do ask questions, do not give them the answers. Instead, ask another question. Let students grapple with the answers as they share aloud. Have conversation time with students on the mat. This opens up so many doors to content knowledge and deeper thinking.

2. When do you use higher-order thinking in your classroom lessons?

   Teachers and students can use higher-order thinking all the time, whether it be at recess while playing or during a math lesson, or during conversation time. It is the questioning and problem-solving processes that encourages higher-order thinking. The opportunities are all around us.

3. Do you pose questions about things that are familiar to students? Does this affect the quality of the response you get from the students?

   Students cannot comment on things that are unfamiliar to them. They must have some background knowledge. Depending on how much background students have, the questions can pick up from there. To find out their level of knowledge, a teacher must simply ask them what they know about this topic. Let the students talk and listen to what they say. Then, the teacher will know where to begin.

4. Do you pose questions about things that students are interested in? Does this affect the quality of the response you get from the students?

   To get students to learn, they must be interested in the topic. When students see that teachers are passionate about something, they will be passionate about learning it, too. Again, the teacher must model inquisitiveness. Learning should be fun for everyone, even the teacher.

5. Can all your students think critically and creatively?

   All students can think critically. They think differently from one another. Some seem to do it better, but it is probably because they have background knowledge about what is being talked about.

6. Can your students solve problems, brainstorm ideas, analyze images, express their opinions, and compare and contrast two concrete objects?

   Yes, all our young students can do these things. Even struggling students can display higher-order thinking. It may be on the playground. It might be in the classroom. There is no difference in the ability to think. All students have the ability to think on higher levels.

7. What is your advice to other teachers? How can a teacher marry the use of higher-order thinking with developmentally appropriate activities?

Many teachers do not want to change the way they teach because it is hard to change. However, we have found that this way of teaching is actually easier than the traditional teaching methods we were taught in college. It takes less planning because it comes naturally to us.

How to Maintain Higher-Order Thinking in the Classroom

It is not only important to begin using higher-order thinking with young students; it is also imperative that teachers continue using higher-order thinking as students get older and advance through the grades. Below is a list of ways that teachers can continue to use higher-order thinking.

- **Let students ask questions.** The most important key to higher-order thinking is getting students to ask questions. Some students will readily ask questions. If students come from environments where teachers have told them that they ask too many questions, they will naturally hesitate to do so. But even in the worst situations, students can be rehabilitated to be inquirers. It is up to each teacher to train students to be inquirers. Teachers train by modeling inquiry for students and can pose those types of questions for students. They can set up scenarios of exploration at the beginning of a lesson or place something in front of students and let them touch, observe, and listen. Then, stick around to hear the questions that students ask about it. When the teacher hears a good question, the teacher needs to point it out, write it on the board, and make a big deal about it. This encourages students to inquire.

- **Allow students to solve the problems.** When a problem poses itself, instead of giving the solution or fixing the problem, the teacher can ask students what they think should be done. If the teacher knows the answer, he or she should "play dumb." If the teacher really does not know the answer, he or she should admit it and be a learner alongside the students. Teachers can show students that they care about learning, too.

- **Remember that questions motivate thinking.** One way to begin developing higher-order thinking in students is by asking questions. The key to asking those higher-order questions is based in the *language*. There is a language to higher-order thinking. Higher-order thinking is based on a specific vocabulary: *opinion, analysis, synthesis, compare/contrast, judge*, etc. It is rare for a teacher to ask a kindergarten student to "analyze this picture." However, that does not mean that he or she cannot get them to analyze the picture. The teacher can ask the students what they think the picture means or to explain what they think about the picture.

- **Know that questions should be thought-provoking.** Instead of asking the recall questions of *who, what*, and *where*, try asking questions that begin with *why* or *what if*. This stimulates good conversations in a classroom. The teacher can create an environment where students can make mistakes without being criticized. Students can be encouraged to explain their thinking when solving a problem. This helps students to analyze their own thinking and teachers to understand their learning styles.

- **Encourage learning, not just knowing.** In order for the teacher to accomplish this, he or she must train the students to be comfortable with failure and ambiguity. The classroom environment must be one that is safe. Students must see their teachers taking risks. Teachers should teach the value in "failure." If an experiment goes awry, the teacher can point out the things learned from the botched experiment. As said previously in this chapter, the process is more important than the final answer.

Conclusion

Many people wonder at which point higher-order thinking skills can be taught to students. In some circles, there is a belief that students need to be older to think critically and creatively. However, even young children can problem-solve, which is a higher-order thinking skill. In fact, researchers and practitioners agree that beginning early is both possible and beneficial.

The human brain is made to grow and learn. The goal of every good teacher is that students learn and grow intellectually. Classroom environment, enrichment/challenge, and feedback are key to making this happen. Higher-order thinking fits within these realms because it encourages more advanced thinking. And, it can be used with all students, regardless of age. The key is using higher-order thinking within developmentally appropriate activities. Beginning in kindergarten, teachers can encourage inquiry. It is natural for these young learners to wonder about everything. Older students need a safe environment so that they can risk posing questions without fear of ridicule or failure. Teachers need to lead the inquiry process by modeling how to question in the classroom. The most important thing to remember is that the problem-solving process itself—and not necessarily just the finding of the solution—encourages brain growth.

Let's Think and Discuss

1. In the past, what biases have you had regarding the use of higher-order thinking?

2. In what ways can you marry the use of higher-order thinking with developmentally appropriate activities in your classroom?

3. If a teacher does not use higher-order thinking skills with his or her students, how could you encourage him or her to do so?

Chapter 4

Platforms for Higher-Order Thinking

We don't have time for higher-order thinking when we have to teach content.

Isn't visual literacy something only done in language arts class?

Mathematical reasoning will come naturally to students as we practice solving math problems.

Scientific inquiry only takes place once a year during the science fair.

The ways in which higher-order thinking is used can vary depending on what content is being taught. For example, the ways in which students need to think about mathematics can be somewhat different from how they need to think about social studies. However, the very opposite can be true as well. Using higher-order thinking in the content areas is very likely to overlap, too. Students can use inquiry in both science and history. On the following pages, a few broad umbrella topics that are embedded in higher-order thinking skills are discussed. These topics include the following:

- Historical thinking

- Visual literacy

- Mathematical reasoning

- Scientific inquiry

Historical Thinking

History is so much more than a collection of facts. The ultimate goal of studying history is the pursuit of understanding. How does one time period lead into another time period? What caused the next event to happen? How is history pieced together to make a long story? Unfortunately, many history teachers approach the teaching of history by first providing the knowledge of facts as the basis for understanding history. Dates, people, and places are gathered first. Then, students are asked to think about it. When history is taught like this, it is no surprise that students see history as just a collection of fragmented dates that have no connection. When facts are taught in isolation, they have very little meaning, and students cannot see continuity and change over time. It is not that content is unimportant; rather, the problem is that many well-intentioned history teachers teach *only* content and omit the rich historical thinking that leads to a true understanding of history.

Social studies and history classes are the perfect venue for teaching and using higher-order thinking skills, and this type of thinking goes way beyond enabling students to give an opinion about an event from history. Historical thinking refers to a set of reasoning skills that are developed as a result of studying history and lead to true historical understanding, as opposed to knowing facts about history. Sam Wineburg, a professor of education at Stanford University, says that historical thinking involves comparing different stories and weighing different perspectives (Wineburg and Schneider 2009). To really understand a historical event, historians use the clues gathered from the way people lived at the time, important primary sources surrounding the event, and their background knowledge. They look at the *why* of history much more than the *what* of history. Understanding why something happened and how it impacted history naturally tells what happened and leads to a deeper understanding of history, and a deeper understanding of today. Looking at *why* takes learning to a higher level.

Even some of the very best teachers feel that they must begin teaching with a collection of facts. These teachers argue that students cannot be asked to consider complex concepts about which they have no prior knowledge. And, while that sounds like a good argument, it *can* be a flawed argument. *All* students have some degree of background knowledge, be it large or small. Contrary to popular belief, students are not blank slates. This prior knowledge can be referred to as *capital*—something that has value. Some students have more academic capital than others because their parents were able to provide them with enriching experiences. Others have cultural capital because they have traveled to foreign countries and have a cultural point of view. For example, suppose a teacher refers to cupcakes in a lesson. Some English language learners may never have heard of cupcakes, but they might know about cake or sweet breads. These students bring what they know to the table. If a teacher wants to introduce the topic of revolutions, particularly ones in Europe, he or she can begin by talking about wars today. Every time a teacher asks students to think about something, students are bringing something to the table. Teachers must activate what the students already know and scaffold for what they do not know. It is important for teachers to know students' experiences so they can plan appropriate instruction.

True historical understanding involves inductive thinking—we know the outcome. For example, we know that World War II happened. We need to find out what caused it to happen. Historical thinking involves piecing together tidbits from different points in time to complete the story. Historical understanding is important because past events still have repercussions today.

Often, history and social studies teachers are very skilled at teaching content. What needs to be improved upon is the teaching of thinking within the content. How can teachers encourage the use of higher-order thinking in history class? They can begin by finding out what prior knowledge and exposure students have to the topic.

Teachers can model higher-order thinking while using primary source documents by showing students how to examine a primary source. The following are some steps that show how teachers can model higher-order thinking while using a primary source document:

1. Scan the primary source document for important dates, names, and places.

2. Talk aloud to let students know what you are thinking.

3. Think about the context in which the source was produced. What was the situation at that time?

4. Read the document closely, asking questions aloud as you read.

5. Compare the document to other sources from the time. What is different? What is the same? Did you find conflicting information?

6. Realize that there will always be remaining questions after careful analysis. For these very reasons, historians do not always agree.

The expectation is that after teachers have modeled how to "read" primary source documents, students will learn how to do it, too. To make this more structured, teachers can list it out as a step-by-step process, as it is shown above.

Once students can read primary source documents, teachers can set up scenarios where students have to choose the most reliable source out of two choices. This involves teachers helping students understand that studying history is similar to being a detective. It sparks questioning in students. And, it teaches them that questioning is both valued and beneficial.

To begin using historical thinking in the classroom, use the following steps:

1. Show students a primary source document with which they are not familiar.

2. Give students time to read it closely.

3. Ask questions that go beyond identifying a primary source instead of making students think about the purpose of the primary source and how it fits within a time frame. This type of questioning involves looking at the bias, ego, and intentions of the creator of the primary source. These questions can include:

   • Why was this primary source created? Defend your answer.

   • What does this primary source say about the time period in which it was created?

4. If students do not give satisfying answers, and they may not at first, push them by asking why and making them identify the reasons behind their answers.

Primary and secondary sources are excellent choices for getting students to think historically. Keeping the general rule of finding out the "why" behind the creation of primary sources is key.

Visual Literacy

It has often been said that there is a difference between looking and seeing, between watching and observing. To move from simply looking to seeing implies that thinking is involved. The same goes for watching and observing. Observing implies that one is taking in information, possibly storing it for future use. There are so many things to see and observe in our world today, and these images are used to communicate messages to us. Look around. Whether you are walking through the airport, driving down the street, surfing the Web, or watching television, images are everywhere. These images are talking to us, spreading their messages. Those who created these visual images have a point they are trying to make. Visual texts can include maps, advertisements, graphs, videos, pictures, calendars, diagrams, signs, symbols, and time lines, just to name a few.

Visual literacy is the ability to understand communications composed of visual images *and* the ability to use visual imagery to communicate to others. When students can translate meaning from images or gestures, they are using visual decoding skills. When students can express their thoughts and ideas in visual form, they are using visual encoding skills. Thibault and Walbert (2010) say that "visual literacy is the ability to see, to understand, and ultimately to think, create, and communicate graphically. . . the visually literate viewer looks at an image carefully, critically, and with an eye for the intentions of the image's creator" (2010, 1). In simplistic form, visual literacy is the *reading and writing* of visual texts.

Some view visual literacy as being a skill strongly tied to language arts because it uses the term *literacy*. However, visual literacy is an important skill used in all content areas. To understand scientific diagrams, a student must be a strong visual reader. In order to grasp key historical events written in a primary source document, a student must be a strong visual reader who knows how to look for clues within the document. Solving a mathematical problem often involves reading and creating visual representations of the problem, which is true to how we solve mathematical problems on a daily basis.

Literacy, in its truest form, crosses through all content areas, and visual literacy is no different.

Being visually literate involves evaluating, applying, and creating conceptual visual representations—all of which are higher-order thinking skills. Visual literacy is important for many reasons. According to Levin (1981), visual literacy is important because images can contain information not found in the texts. Sometimes, images can represent information better than text can. Think about trying to explain to someone where he or she can find a certain location as opposed to showing them the location on a map. It is much easier to use the map to communicate location. Levin also points out that images and graphics can be used as organizational tools that support learning. Think of the many instructional graphic organizers, such as flowcharts, used to summarize and simplify information. Just think of the possible job opportunities for those with strong literacy skills. They understand how to create messages using visual images. Strong visual literacy skills are important for those who desire to work in business, communications, and engineering, just to name a few.

Begin encouraging visual literacy with the following steps:

1. Display an image that you want students to analyze. It is usually best to start with something with which they are familiar, such as a fast-food sign or a billboard from the local community.

2. Ask students the following questions to promote higher-order thinking:

    - What does the sign mean?

    - What were the motives behind making a sign like this?

    - What does the sign creator want you to do?

    - Pretend the sign can talk. What does it say to you?

3. Ask students to improve the visual. This gets students analyzing, evaluating, and creating in order to make it talk better and also improves their visual-writing abilities.

4. Repeat the process with a visual that is not familiar to students. Let them practice these same skills on the new image. It might be tough at first, so continue showing familiar images and then switch back to the new image.

The key to improving visual literacy is the same as improving other skills. Students need many opportunities to apply these skills of understanding visuals. The more students practice this, the better visual readers and writers they will become.

Mathematical Reasoning

Many students think of mathematics as a class in which they solve meaningless problems on worksheets instead of training themselves to reason through problems they will encounter in life. These students understand the goal as getting the right answer and fail to realize that the reason for learning mathematics is that we live in a mathematical world. Instead of knowing why answers are true, they memorize the formulas and paths to get the right answers for homework and the test. As a result, these students grow into adults who freeze up when they see a mathematical problem. They cannot recall the formulas or steps to answer those types of questions. As a result, many everyday problems are not resolved. According to the National Council of Teachers of Mathematics (NCTM) (2000), "mathematical competence opens doors to productive futures." Good mathematics teachers will tell you that the goal of their classes is to produce students who use mathematical reasoning so that they can have productive futures and opportunities. But just what does mathematical reasoning look like?

When a student looks at how to solve a mathematical problem and asks himself or herself, *Am I on the right track? Does this make sense?* he or she is using mathematical reasoning. When a student adds two whole numbers, such as *10 + 12 = 7*, and then follows up with the question *Could this be true?* mathematical reasoning is taking place. Both of these students want to reach acceptable solutions, and they are using mathematical reasoning to get there. Whether it be conscious or subconscious, they are asking themselves questions such as *Do I need to create tables, draw pictures, or use calculators?* Mathematical reasoning is the internal process students go through in their heads to think about what steps they need to perform. Much of this mathematical reasoning involves perseverance, or mathematical stamina, as they rethink and re-reason their way through a problem to find what works (Gojak 2010).

Mathematical reasoning supports higher-order thinking. The core of higher-order thinking is good questioning—the type of questioning that pushes students to make connections and explain the reasons behind why an answer is correct or incorrect instead of what the answer is to a question. Open-ended questions can serve this purpose very well. To encourage mathematical reasoning in students, change questions so that students have to make those connections and explain their reasoning. For example, this might be a typical question: *What is the perimeter of the rectangle?* By changing the question, more thinking is required from students. *What happens to the perimeter of the rectangle if the length of two parallel sides is cut in half? Explain your answer.* Another example might ask students to compare two different problems or to find the answer using different kinds of strategies. Better yet, provide students with a problem that contains a false answer, and ask students to explain why the answer is false. All of these scenarios require students to use mathematical reasoning, something that will benefit them throughout their lives.

Questions that promote mathematical reasoning can include:

- What evidence supports your answer?

- How can you show the relationship between . . . ?

- What if . . . ?

- How could you decide . . . ?

- How would you explain the procedures to solve a problem?

- How important is . . . ?

NCTM (2000) has set forth principles and standards for mathematics that include standards for reasoning and proof. The goal of using reasoning is that students will come to the understanding that mathematics is reasonable and makes sense. By having students reason mathematically on a consistent basis, it will become a "habit of mind."

These process standards state that instruction for students in kindergarten through grade 12 should enable students to:

- Recognize reasoning and proof as fundamental aspects of mathematics

- Make and investigate mathematical conjectures

- Develop and evaluate mathematical arguments and proofs

- Select and use various types of reasoning and methods of proof

Use the following tips to help encourage your students to use mathematical reasoning:

- As often as you can, ask "Does this make sense?" as you are solving problems in class. When students think of you, they should envision you *always* asking this question.

- Students need to prove what they are doing. Make students answer the question, *"How do you know?"*

- Be aware of thinking aloud in front of your students. They need to learn to think like mathematicians, so teach them by modeling it. Students will not know how to do it unless you explicitly tell them. As you work, tell them how you are figuring it out. Then, ask them to do it, too.

- Always end a lesson with the *why*. Why do students need to learn this? Give the reasons behind knowing how to perform a mathematical skill. This emphasizes the connections to real life.

- Always have students make connections: math to math, math to self, math to world (Hyde 2006).

- Extend the students' thinking by giving problems that make them apply what you are teaching. It is not enough to solve problems; students must be able to apply them in new contexts.

For some students, mathematical reasoning is intuitive. These students have the natural aptitude for it, even if they are not aware of it. For the students who do not readily use mathematical reasoning, teachers must provide the opportunities for students to practice it.

Scientific Inquiry

Scientific inquiry involves creative questioning of something that can be tested.

"When engaging in inquiry, students describe objects and events, ask questions, construct explanations, test those explanations against current scientific knowledge, and communicate their ideas to others. They identify their assumptions, use critical and logical thinking, and consider alternative explanations" (National Science Education Standards 1996).

The term *inquiry* is at the heart of higher-order thinking because it involves asking questions. According to a study by the National Research Council, "scientific inquiry is the diverse ways in which scientists study the natural world and propose explanations based on the evidence derived from their work. Scientific inquiry also refers to the activities through which students develop knowledge and understanding of scientific ideas, as well as an understanding of how scientists study the natural world" (National Science Education Standards 1996). For scientists, inquiry is not a neat step-by-step process. At times, the results do not answer the questions. The results of an experiment can result in more questions being asked.

A study conducted by Fred Newmann at the University of Wisconsin found schools that used inquiry-based teaching showed significantly higher achievement on challenging tasks (Barron 2008). According to his research, inquiry-based learning had more impact on student achievement than student background or any other variable.

Inquiry learning is not focused on getting the right answer. Rather, it is about developing an inquisitive mind. In an inquiry-based classroom, the goal is for students to develop skills, develop their own questions, formulate their hypotheses, design their experiments, test their hypotheses, conduct their experiments (make observations), and draw their conclusions. Students should be able to explain their experiments and conclusions to others in a way that is replicable and understandable. They should also be able to respond to questions about their findings. All of this is tied to higher-order thinking.

The inquiry-based classroom contrasts with rote and fact-based learning, as well as memorization (merely for the sake of memorization). The teacher does not impart knowledge, but creates an environment in which students learn for themselves through their own inquisitiveness. Inquiry-based classrooms encourage questions like *why, what if,* or *is it possible?* Rich questioning is the heart and soul of scientific inquiry. Teachers can ask open-ended questions such as, *What made you think of that?* or make statements like, *Tell me more about how you arrived at that conclusion.* They respond to students by paraphrasing what the student said as a way to elicit discussion on the question. They encourage students to think for themselves.

The following are the five essential features of inquiry outlined in Inquiry and the National Science Education Standards (National Science Education Standards 1996):

- Learner engages in scientifically oriented questions

- Learner gives priority to evidence in responding to questions

- Learner formulates explanations from evidence

- Learner connects explanations to scientific knowledge

- Learner communicates and justifies explanations

Some question stems to use that promote inquiry can include:

- What might you predict the outcome of . . . ?

- How can you support the reasoning behind . . .?

- What are the factors that might influence . . . ?

- What are three different ways to classify . . . ?

The ultimate goal in scientific inquiry is for students to learn to think like scientists. And this skill, which promotes questioning, will be an invaluable tool that will naturally affect how students learn and process information as thinkers.

Conclusion

Higher-order thinking skills are at the very heart and center of historical thinking, visual literacy, mathematical reasoning, and scientific inquiry. All of these methods necessitate students to employ higher-order thinking. Historical thinking is founded in reasoning skills that analyze events, people, and sources from history. Visual literacy is the ability to read and write using visual texts. Mathematical reasoning goes beyond the act of simply finding a solution to understanding the "why" of the solution and making sense of mathematics. And finally, scientific inquiry provides the opportunity for students to develop skills, develop their own questions, formulate their hypotheses, design their experiments, test their hypotheses, conduct their experiments (make observations), and draw their conclusions. Historical thinking, visual literacy, mathematical reasoning, and scientific inquiry can be tied to thinking in specific content areas, but they often reach beyond those content areas because that is what good thinking does—it transforms the way students look at and solve problems.

Let's Think and Discuss

1. In what ways have you used historical thinking, visual literacy, mathematical reasoning, or scientific inquiry in your classroom?

2. How do you foresee other ways in which you can incorporate some of these methods into your teaching?

3. How receptive do you believe your students will be to using these methods to learn in your classroom? Explain.

Chapter 5

Strategies for Higher-Order Thinking Skills

There are many strategies that promote higher-order thinking skills. This chapter contains just a sampling of ways to infuse curriculum with specific strategies that promote higher-order thinking skills. These strategies include questioning strategies, problem-solving strategies, decision-making strategies, idea-generating strategies and activities, thinking organizers, creative strategies, project-based learning, and open-ended tasks.

Questioning Strategies

Revised Bloom's Taxonomy

In 1956, educator Benjamin Bloom worked with a group of educational psychologists to classify levels of cognitive thinking. Bloom's Taxonomy has been used in classrooms for more than 50 years as a hierarchy of questions that progresses from less to more complex. The progression allows teachers to identify the levels at which students are thinking. It can also provide a framework for introducing a variety of questions to all students.

In 2001, cognitive psychologist Lorin Anderson, a former student of Benjamin Bloom, led a group of researchers to revise and update the taxonomy to make it relevant to the 21st century. There are several main changes to the taxonomy. One involves changing some nouns to verbs. For example, instead of *knowledge* (a noun), the word is *remembering* (a verb).

Revised Bloom's Taxonomy
Remembering (formerly Knowledge)
Retrieving previously learned material by recall
Verbs: tell, recall, what, who, when, where, which, list, match, label
Products: worksheet, quiz, reproduction, list
Understanding (formerly Comprehension)
Constructing meaning from oral, written, and graphic messages through interpreting, exemplifying, classifying, summarizing, inferring, comparing, and explaining
Verbs: compare, contrast, demonstrate, outline, classify, explain, summarize
Products: story problem, summary, collection, outline, report, diagram

Revised Bloom's Taxonomy *(cont.)*

Applying (formerly Apply)

Carrying out or using a procedure through executing or implementing

Verbs: organize, solve, identify, interview, experiment, build, construct, plan, model

Products: scrapbook, puzzle, illustration, experiment, interview, journal, map, advertisement, recipe

Analyzing (formerly Analyze)

Breaking material into constituent parts, determining how the parts relate to one another and to an overall structure or purpose through differentiating, organizing, and attributing

Verbs: dissect, inspect, infer, categorize, discover, classify, survey, examine

Products: questionnaire, spreadsheet, survey, chart, categorize, investigation

Evaluating (formerly Synthesis)

Making judgments based on criteria and standards through checking and critiquing

Verbs: award, criticize, justify, dispute, decide, recommend, measure, assess, value, appraise

Products: editorial, debate, film, recommendation, review

Creating (formerly Evaluate)

Putting elements together to form a coherent or functional whole; reorganizing elements into a new pattern or structure through generating, planning, or producing

Verbs: elaborate, create, improve, design, modify, maximize, propose, change, adapt, originate

Products: invention, newspaper, song, collage, solution, play, creative story

(Anderson, David and Krathwohl 2001)

Also, the hierarchy of the last two levels of Bloom's Taxonomy changed from *evaluation* being the highest form of thinking to *creating* as the highest form of thinking, the rationale being that the evaluation of something that is already present is necessary before one can create something new. The act of creating is viewed as a more difficult task than evaluating. The figure below shows the difference between the last two levels of Bloom's Taxonomy.

Fig. 5.1 Original Bloom's vs. Revised Bloom's Taxonomy

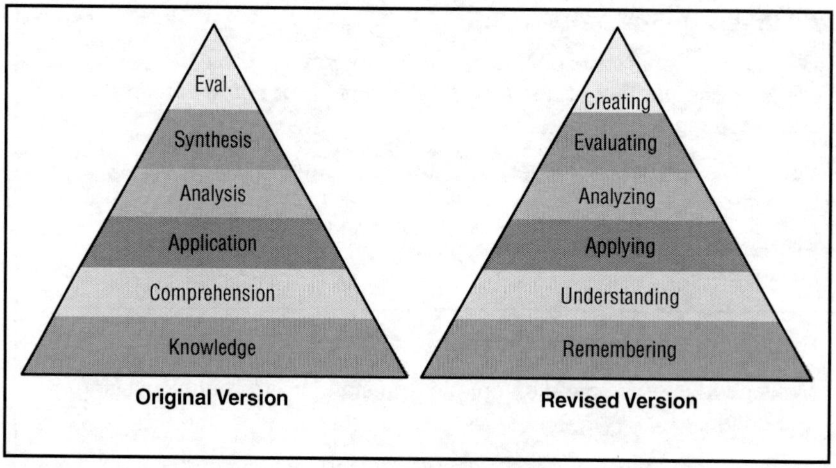

In addition, Anderson, David and Krathwohl (2001) points out the ways the taxonomy intersects with different levels of knowledge such as factual, conceptual, procedural, and metacognitive.

Some teachers view Bloom's Taxonomy as a ladder. They think all students have to begin at the bottom with remembering questions and work their way progressively up to the creating questions. Other teachers believe that the gifted students should answer the higher-order questions, on-grade-level students should answer the mid-level questions, and struggling students should answer the lower-order questions. While there is nothing inherently wrong with these two practices, each one should be used sparingly when the situation requires it. Perhaps the best way to view this taxonomy is to think of it as a feedback loop. Maureen Donohue-Smith (2006) views Bloom's Taxonomy as a feedback loop. She says, "The answers to higher-order questions either support or challenge the questioner's data and thus cycle back to a potential reconfiguration of prior knowledge. Students may question facts, rethink interpretations, or challenge generalizations at any point" (2006, 43).

Some people view Bloom's lower-order questions as inferior to the higher-order questions. This leads to the misconception that students do not need facts, when in fact they do need them. The problem has been that some teachers rely solely on the teaching of facts because it is more natural to ask lower-level questions and assign lower-level activities. All of this is done out of a desire for students to gain the necessary information. However, instead of the goal being the memorization and regurgitation of facts, it is more important for 21st century thinkers to know how to *access* those facts to support their thinking. Very few people can remember the millions of facts presented throughout the years in school. That does not mean that facts should not be taught. The point is not to prevent students from knowing facts; however, the move needs to be shifted from remembering the facts to knowing how to access and use the facts when necessary. Every 21st century thinker needs to be able to access the facts. Students should be able to sort through the most important pieces of information because all facts do not carry the same weight.

Interestingly, Sam Wineburg and Jack Schneider (2009) have a view of critical thinking using an inverted Bloom's Taxonomy pyramid. They say that the way to critical thinking, at least in history class, is not to assemble all the facts and then make up their mind about what they think. Instead, it is more important to "determine what questions to ask in order to generate new knowledge" (2004). In their article "Inverting Bloom's Taxonomy," Wineburg and Schneider give the example of AP students analyzing a proclamation by President Benjamin Harrison in 1892. The students read the document to find out the *what*. What did the document say? The document declared Discovery Day in honor of Christopher Columbus. Then, the students passed judgment on the document, commenting mainly on their opinion of celebrating what Columbus did. Then, graduate students who specialized in French colonialism and the Meiji

Restoration were given the same document. They did not have any more background on Columbus than the AP students. They read the document for the *why*. Why would Harrison have produced a document like this? What was going on at the time this document was produced? By reading the document with questions in mind, they then could access the knowledge about the time period to fully understand what this document was all about.

Wineburg and Schneider say, "In history, as in other disciplines, the aim is not merely to collect what is known, but to learn how to think about problems in a new way" (2009, 31). In teachers' efforts to have students use the levels of Bloom's Taxonomy to think critically, they must be aware that simply having students pass judgment on something does not really mean they have used critical thinking to its best measure. The goal of critical thinking is not just about thinking, but to acquire new knowledge.

Make no mistake—the ultimate objective in classrooms is to use higher-order thinking not because it is superior to facts, but because higher-order thinking encompasses lower-order thinking. The value of higher-order thinking is immense, because all levels of thinking are utilized. To be able to analyze, students need to understand and comprehend the facts. Higher-order thinking trains students for real-world application outside the classroom. It involves a series of related problems that contain important facts to solve instead of just a series of related facts to memorize. These activities will support students as they grow into adults and make decisions, such as which cell phone plan is better, which health care plan to choose, which college to attend, or to what retirement plan to contribute. Students must be able to acquire the facts to make a good decision, accessing higher-order thinking skills. The goal is building educated learners, and that happens by using higher-order thinking.

Bloom's Taxonomy can serve as a gauge for teachers to use when assigning activities or asking questions to help purposefully plan for higher-order thinking. There is no formula or right way to use the revised Bloom's Taxonomy in each lesson. What matters is knowing the needs of students. At times, students need to begin with lower-order questions so they can build a foundation to support higher-order thinking. This can even be true for very bright students. Other times, students can jump directly to higher-order thinking and then investigate the facts. However, the evaluating question might need to be scaffolded for language for struggling students and for English language learners. These practices support the idea of Bloom's Taxonomy being a feedback loop. All of these questions work together to provide a solid foundation of thinking.

For example, a lesson about bats could help primary students make connections to other mammals if questions are asked, such as why they are unique; how they fit within the food chain, web, and ecosystem; what happens if the population gets too high, and how this changes the balance of things. A lesson on bats geared toward upper elementary students can support understanding of the implications of a diminishing bat population.

Bloom's Taxonomy has withstood the test of time as a solid structure for questioning. At the same time, it has also been strengthened by the changes as a result of strong research. Teachers often find it both easy to understand and friendly to use. For these reasons and many more, Bloom's Taxonomy is a viable questioning strategy that can promote higher-order thinking in the classroom.

The Williams Model

Frank Williams developed a program designed to enrich curriculum for all students in the early 1970s. The Williams model has three dimensions. The first dimension outlines subject-matter content such as mathematics, language, science, social science, art, and music. The second dimension shows 18 strategies for teaching. These include tolerance for ambiguity, creative writing skills, and analogies. The third and final dimension focuses on student behaviors. These eight student behaviors demonstrate students' creativity. All eight of these levels are an extension of Bloom's *creating* (formerly *synthesis*) level of thinking. Four levels (fluency, flexibility, originality, and elaboration) are cognitive, or intellectual, processes. Four levels (curiosity, risk taking, complexity, and imagination) are affective, or feeling, processes.

A natural outcome of practicing creative behavior results is being more creative. The cultivation of creativity has many benefits among adolescents such as reduced dropout rates and increased student motivation (Sautter 1994). It can protect children from stress (Honigh 2000). It helps a person "avoid boredom, resolve personal conflict, cope with increasing consumer choice, accept complexity and ambiguity, make independent judgments, use leisure time constructively, and adjust to the rapid development of new knowledge" (Strom 2000, 59). According to Fryer (1996), adolescents must learn to think creatively so they can keep up with the technology changes in society. The Williams model can be an effective instrument in producing creative behaviors in our students and thus making our students more creative individuals.

Many teachers might find this model overwhelming because of its breadth. However, by forming questions that support Williams's proposed student outcomes, students can learn to think more creatively. The following are Williams's proposed student outcomes:

Fluency—Questions generate many ideas, related answers, or choices.

Flexibility—Questions encourage flexibility and seek to change everyday objects so that an array of categories is generated. Detours are taken, and sizes, shapes, quantities, time limits, requirements, objectives, or dimensions are varied.

Elaboration—Questions expand, enlarge, enrich, or embellish possibilities that build on prior ideas or thoughts.

Originality—Questions promote originality and seek new ideas by suggesting unusual twists to change content or to generate clever responses.

Curiosity—Questions promote curiosity and allow students to follow a hunch, question alternatives, ponder outcomes, and wonder about options.

Risk-taking—Questions deal with the unknown by asking students to take chances, try new things, or experiment with new ideas.

Complexity—Questions create structure in an unstructured setting. They can also build a logical order in a given situation.

Imagination—Questions encourage imagination and help students visualize possibilities, build images in the mind, picture new objects, and reach beyond the practical limits.

Teachers can take these student outcomes and design questions that encourage these behaviors. This is referred to as Williams's Taxonomy. As with taxonomies that have many levels of questions, teachers should not strive to design questions for every level. This dilutes the curriculum. Teachers should choose levels that support what needs to be taught and then design questions. The example below shows questions that use five of the eight levels of Williams's Taxonomy.

Desert Ecosystem Example

Fluency—In two minutes, list the living things that can survive in the desert.

Elaboration—The desert can be 115 degrees Fahrenheit (or 46 degrees Celsius) during the day and 32 degrees Fahrenheit or (0 degrees Celsius) at night. Explain how life forms survive in the deserts with such extreme temperatures.

Originality—What adaptations would a polar bear have to make to survive in the desert?

Risk-taking—If snakes became extinct in the desert, what would be the worst consequence?

Imagination—Describe the contents of a completely new ecosystem, including what living things would populate it, the vegetation, and the possible location.

The Socratic Method

Inquiry is at the heart of the Socratic seminar, Socratic dialogue, or Socratic method, as it is most commonly called. This strategy is named after the philosopher Socrates, who used a broad form of questioning with his students. Each question that is answered predetermines the next question. Socrates used it to show his students the error of their thinking. Since the time Socrates used inquiry to promote thinking, the Socratic method has changed somewhat through the years. Today, this method is used primarily as a process of inductive questioning, through small steps, with knowledge as the goal. In a classroom, a teacher can use a set of questions to provoke students to think about something. The questions push students to examine what they know with the result of them analyzing a topic in depth.

By using the Socratic method, learners can come to value and recognize good questions while also improving upon a thoughtful method of thinking. Students become more curious about the topic. They experience the joy of discovery. Students also get immediate feedback, and teachers can monitor student understanding by making adjustments, clarifying, and correcting misgivings immediately instead of waiting until the end of the unit test to find out that students did not understand the material. For the teacher, teaching is more interesting because he or she can quickly glean the thought processes of the students. Classes will respond differently, so even content-area teachers who teach the same class multiple times daily will not grow bored with student responses. This method also allows teachers to see student potential, as some students might pose exceptional questions that might not happen during a regular class.

Some might mistakenly think that the Socratic method requires very little preparation. On the contrary, to implement the Socratic method in class, there is strategic teacher preparation involved. First, teachers should make a list of good questions to ask and mentally go through the conversation beforehand. The first questions are designed to show what students understand about the topic so the teacher knows where to begin. The questions need to follow a logical sequence of steps that takes learners from one point of knowledge to another. The questions should follow a logical path that supports what the teacher wants students to learn. These questions should be specific enough to lead students to the desired understanding while also engaging students so that curiosity is piqued.

If students answer incorrectly, a teacher must decide whether students need to know why their answer is wrong or not. Not all questions will be the best or even appropriate, so teachers need to be open to the idea of fine-tuning how they question their students.

Dr. Richard Paul is the director of research and professional development at the Center for Critical Thinking and chair of the National Council for Excellence in Critical Thinking. He has classified Socratic questions into six different categories which are listed in the figure on the following page. Within each category, there are questions that support the area of focus. It is the basic practice that, while these do not follow a hierarchy of questions, they can lead one to another (Paul and Elder 2002).

Socratic Questions

Questions that clarify	• What is an example of...? • Can you explain...? • How would you say this in your own words? • What is the right way to define this?
Questions that probe assumptions	• Why do you think this way about...? • What are your assumptions? • What do you believe to be true? • What else could we believe about this?
Questions that look for reasons and evidence	• What makes you believe this? • How do we know this is true? • What else do we need to know? • What would make you change your mind about...?
Questions about perspectives and viewpoints	• Whose viewpoint is this? • What bias does this have? • What is another view about...? • How many more perspectives could there be about...?
Questions that look at consequences	• How does this affect...? • Why is this important? • What effect can this have on...? • If this is true, then what else might be true?
Questions about the question	• What does this question mean? • Is this a good question? • Why was this question asked? • What does this have to do with our lives?

(Adapted from Paul and Elder 2002)

Depth of Knowledge

Depth of Knowledge (DOK) is a scale of cognitive demand that uses questions, tasks, and products ranked at four levels. The scale is adapted from the work of Norman Webb at the University of Wisconsin.

The levels of thinking are differentiated by the complexity of mental processing required. Some equate the idea of difficulty with complexity. However, the difficulty of a question is usually assessed by how many students can answer the question, do the task, or create the product. Can students find the area of a room? If many students can do this, then it is an easy task. If not many students can do this, then it can be ranked as a difficult task. Depth of Knowledge relies on complexity, not difficulty. It focuses on the complexity of the mental process that it takes for students to answer questions, perform tasks, or create products.

Level 3 is strategic thinking and requires a deep understanding of the story, the character, and humankind. It is open-ended, but students must take what they know about the character and put together probable events and experiences that impacted that character. Level 2 is more complex than Level 1 because students are comparing the character to themselves, so their answers will vary. Level 1 only asks students to describe the character based on what they have read, so it is a simple recall question.

The four levels of thinking are as follows:

- **Level 1** is described as the recall level, where facts, information, or procedures are recalled. It requires the lowest level of thinking.

- **Level 2** is described as the skill or concept level. Typically, students classify, organize, estimate, collect, display, observe, and compare data. They use the information they know. This level requires deeper thinking than does Level 1.

- **Level 3** is characterized by strategic thinking. Reasoning, planning, and making conjectures are typical at this level. The open-ended tasks are not necessarily what makes this level a higher-order thinking activity. Higher-order thinking comes into play when students have to defend the reason for selecting their answers. Students draw conclusions, support their conclusions with evidence, or determine which concept to apply to solve a problem.

- **Level 4** is described as extended thinking and is the highest level of thinking. It is characterized by complex reasoning by which students make interdisciplinary connections. More often than not, activities at this level take a prolonged period of time. However, be aware that just because a project takes an extended period of time to complete it does not mean that it is a Level 4 task. Level 4 requires an investigation of some sort with a project showing the results of the complex thinking involved. The following Level 4 activity can be added to the example on characteristics of a character.

Look at five of your favorite stories, television shows, or movies and choose a character from each one. Combine characteristics from those five characters to create one character that could be friends with the main character in the story you are reading. First, detail what characteristics you would use from each character. Then, draw a picture of this new character and make notes on the page that show why this character would be a likely friend of the main character. What does he or she think? How does he or she act? What would he or she say? What is his or her personality like? Be sure to show this character in detail and be ready to explain why this new character is perfect as a friend to the main character as well as how the story would change with this newly added character.

The key to the different levels of thinking is not necessarily in the verbs that are used; rather, it is in the depth of thinking that is demanded. What comes after the verbs classifies the level of thinking. For example, there are some verbs that do identify with a lower depth of thinking such as *recall* and *identify*. However, the verbs *describe* and *explain* could be used with different levels depending on what needs to be described and explained. The verbs *must* be considered in context. Consider the following example:

Level 1—*Describe* the main character in the story.

Level 2—*Describe* how you are both similar to and different from the character in the story.

Level 3—*Describe* the possible events that could have led to how the character came to be this way and give reasons for your answer.

Similarly to Bloom's Taxonomy, Depth of Knowledge levels can be cumulative. For example, Level 3 and Level 4 questions and activities often will contain Levels 1 and 2. When planning lessons, try to use more of the Levels 3 and 4, which promote higher-order thinking. Decide what students will research and what final project or product they will produce to show what they have learned in a creative way. These activities should incorporate interdisciplinary activities when possible.

Problem-Solving Strategies

Problem-Based Learning

Problem-based learning is a problem-solving strategy that engages students in solving a *real-life or lifelike* problem. These problems can range from students breaking the dress code to establishing safe evacuation routes for hurricane warnings. This strategy is known for its group work along with independent investigations and inquiry. According to James Rhem (1998), problem-based learning "orients students toward *meaning-making* over *fact-collecting*. They learn via contextualized problem sets and situations" (1998, 1). Problem-based learning as we know it today was first used in the 1950s at Case Western Reserve University. It is described as "a curriculum development and instructional system that simultaneously develops both problem-solving strategies and disciplinary knowledge bases and skills by placing students in the active role of problem solvers confronted with an ill-structured problem that mirrors real-world problems" (Finkle and Torp 1995, 1). Even before the 1950s, John Dewey had the right idea about learning. In the 1930s, Dewey (1916) said that school should be lifelike instead of merely preparing students for life. It has been said that using a problem-based approach to learning may be one of the best ways to understand concepts within a subject area (Barell 2003). Teachers who use a problem-based approach in the classroom not only help students grasp particular concepts but they also pave the way for future learning. Once students learn how to solve one problem, they can transfer that knowledge to solve more problems (Bransford, Franks, and Sherwood 1986). An added benefit is that students remember what they learn because they have opportunities to apply the concepts in more complex ways.

Problem-based learning gives students the opportunity to collaborate with their classmates as they study the issues surrounding a certain problem. They use information they find through research to synthesize viable solutions. The amount of direct instruction in a problem-based classroom is very limited, so students have to take on the responsibility for their own learning. The teacher's role is much like a coach. He or she presents the problematic situation, becomes the subject-matter expert, acts as a resource guide and consultant, and serves as a co-investigator who keeps the students on task. The teacher asks questions like, *Why? What do you mean? How do you know that is true?* He or she questions students' logic and gives hints about erroneous reasoning and models critical thinking so that students will begin to ask the same kinds of questions of one another. The student's role is that of a participant who grapples with the complexity of the situation while investigating and resolving the problem from the inside out.

Think about this scenario as a student in today's classroom:

> *Vandalism is on the rise in your school. Lockers have been broken into, students' belongings have been stolen, furniture has been scratched, and walls have been written on during school hours. The school has decided to implement safety measures. Hall passes will be strictly enforced, and no one will be allowed to leave the cafeteria during lunch. These rules seem extreme to you. You feel that innocent students are being punished for what only a few do. There has to be a better way to stop the vandals. What can you do?*

Your teacher allows you to work in groups to generate possible ideas or solutions to this problem. You decide to write a petition, form volunteer patrols, and survey students. You identify available information related to this problem by reviewing school policies, viewing a sample petition, and looking at parts of the school that have been vandalized. You identify issues that need to be investigated further—how to form patrols, what other schools are doing, and how to write a survey. Your group finds resources to consult, like policies from other schools and sample surveys. Group members are assigned the tasks above and information is gathered. Finally, your group presents your solution to the school board. This is problem-based learning.

There are many reasons for using problem-based learning with students. First, we know that our minds are capable of thinking through complex situations, which promotes higher-level thinking skills. Research says that it is the complex challenges that develop our intellect and ability to think productively (Caine and Caine 1997; Diamond and Hopson 1998). These types of problems do not provide just one right answer. Students are forced into thinking both critically and creatively as they seek to find solutions to problems.

Problem-based learning also increases motivation in students. Recently, some professors at the college level have begun to restructure their course work around problem-based learning. They do this by taking the final exam and working backward to structure the course around a problem that teaches the key concepts they want their students to learn. They freely admit that it is a lot of work to do this but that the results of both student and teacher engagement are well worth it. In fact, they dare say that none of their colleagues have gone back to lecture after using problem-based learning (Rhem 1998). Students see that the outcome of their work can make a real difference in society. It shows that what they do in school can have an impact in the real world, and this builds student confidence.

This type of learning provides opportunities for students to work with others in collaborative groups, which in turn prepares them for their future workplaces where teamwork is both valued and required. In a successful problem-based learning activity, students must listen to one another, synthesize information, and work together. For some students, this can be difficult. Some teachers feel more daunted by this classroom structure than anything else. It does take patience and strategic planning on the teacher's part to train students to work effectively together. Typically, no one has trouble working with others who respect their opinions, listen to their ideas, and try to compromise in one way or another. The problems arise when the exact opposite is true. While it can be a bother to put out fires all day long, providing students with the encouragement, strategies, and experiences of dealing with difficult people is invaluable. Problem-based learning provides the perfect avenue to teach students how to work with others.

While collaborating, great ideas can flow freely. Brainstorming with others brings out creative ideas that might not have been evident if students had been working alone. Problem-based learning is continual brainstorming of what the problem is and how it can be solved. As one student shares, it might spark an idea in another student. It teaches students to appreciate other viewpoints and ideas.

Problem-based learning provides students the chance to develop strong work ethics. So much work, energy, and thinking goes into solving problems. Strategies are generated for identifying and defining the problem, gathering information, analyzing data, and building and testing the hypothesis. All of these steps are important life skills that train students to be hard workers.

Finally, problem-based learning is active. A problem-solving context is the best way to acquire information (Tyler 1949). As students struggle to figure out a problem and apply what they are learning, they are more likely to remember the key concepts taught in that lesson. The way that students are engaged in learning information is similar to the way students will recall it and use it in the future.

A typical problem-based learning lesson has several cycles. These steps can be repeated as many times as necessary to come to a conclusion. The steps are the following:

1. Locate a real-world problem. It is best if this problem can connect to learning standards and goals.

2. Determine facts and find a way for students to enter the problem. Tie it to something that they are interested in. This is called the *hook*.

3. After the problem has been presented, students discuss what they know to be the facts of the problem. They can use a graphic organizer like the KWHLAQ strategy (Barell 2003; 2007a; 2007b) to do this.

4. Students analyze the problem, brainstorm ideas about the problem, and create an exact statement of the problem. This is the hypothesis. The problem statement might sound like this: *How can we . . . in such a way that . . . ?*

5. Students need to identify information necessary to understand the problem and identify resources to be used to gather information.

6. Students find and share information by interviewing, collecting data, and conducting other forms of research. They can revise the problem statement and ask additional questions if necessary.

7. Students develop solutions by studying the information, finding a solution that fits best, and considering the consequences for their solution.

8. Students develop some sort of presentation where they explain, apply, and justify their solution to the problem. Their information can be published for others to see.

KWHLAQ Strategy

K—What do we think we know about the subject?

W—What do we want to know?

H—How will we go about finding answers to our questions?

L—What are we learning on a daily basis, and what have we learned after our culminating projects?

A—How can we apply the major concepts, ideas, principles, and skills to the same subject, to other subjects, and to our lives beyond the classroom?

Q—What new questions do we have now?

(Adapted from Barell 2003; 2007a; 2007b)

While problem-based learning is used predominantly in science classrooms, it can be used in any content area. It is important to remember that the problem should not have a fixed or formulaic solution. There is no one right answer. The problem is generally described as messy and complex in nature. It requires questioning, information gathering, and reflection. Ideas for problem-based learning can come from sources such as television, newspaper articles, and literature. Because students bring their own prior knowledge to develop ideas and formulate those ideas into a hypothesis, these scenarios can be used with most any age group. The high-school level will invariably produce a deeper investigation with more complex results than will a younger classroom. A list of possible topics is provided on the following page.

- childhood obesity

- global warming

- tooth decay

- universal healthcare

- banned books

- fight against hunger and disease

- preventing animal extinction

- increasing tourism

- going green

- funding technology in schools

- civil rights issues

Creative Problem-Solving Model

The CPS model uses a set of six steps to solve problems.

1. Mess finding (locating a problem to which to apply this model)

2. Fact finding (examining details and listing all facts known about a problem)

3. Problem finding (alternative ways to define the problem: "In what ways might we . . . ?")

4. Idea finding (divergent thinking, brainstorming for solutions)

5. Solution finding (idea evaluation)

6. Acceptance finding (implementing the solution)

Over the past five decades, CPS has changed. It is no longer seen as a set of rigid steps that must be followed in order. Today, the steps can be flexible, allowing learners to use them in a more natural way. One example is that these steps can be simplified into three main steps: (1) understanding the problem, (2) generating ideas, and (3) planning for action.

1. Understanding the problem can include first finding the problem and then finding out all the facts about that problem. It can take an amount of time for research and analysis to really know what the problem is all about. This step includes mess finding, fact finding, and problem finding.

2. Generating ideas is the brainstorming part of creative problem solving. Students try to think of many varied and unusual possible solutions to the problem. All ideas are to be written down and taken seriously. Often, some very crazy solutions are given. Sometimes, these end up being the best solutions, so they should never be discarded early on in the brainstorming process. This step, called *idea finding*, should be free of evaluation or criticism.

3. Planning for action is when a solution to the problem is decided upon and implemented. After sitting for a while, this is where the ideas from the previous step can be criticized and evaluated. To narrow down ideas, students can list what is good and what is bad about each of their ideas. This makes students analyze their ideas and think through them. Solution finding and acceptance finding are included in this step.

In a classroom, students work with their classmates to find solutions to problems. Teachers can facilitate small-group discussions and brainstorming sessions with very young students. By modeling and coaching students through CPS, students learn how to take responsibility for their own learning. The teacher's role is much like a coach's in the sense that he or she keeps students on task and helps students to find the problem and generate many possible solutions.

Alex Osborn, the founder of Creative Education Foundation, first used CPS. Osborn believed that using identified steps when solving a problem can encourage creativity. The creative process is guided by using these steps so that in the end, a creative and workable solution is produced. Giving students opportunities to be creative in the classroom can only benefit them in real life, where they will find problems around each corner.

Donald Treffinger says that creative and critical thinking work in harmony in CPS (Treffinger, Isaken, and Stead-Dorval 2006). He views them as complementary ways of thinking instead of polar-opposite thinking activities. Creative thinking works to generate as many ideas as possible. Critical thinking works to focus thinking constructively, narrowing down these ideas to come to a solution. He says that effective problem solvers both generate and focus. In essence, "creativity requires constant shifting, blender pulses of both divergent thinking and convergent thinking, to combine new information with old and forgotten ideas. Highly creative people are very good at marshalling their brains into bilateral mode, and the more creative they are, the more they dual-activate" (Bronson and Merryman 2010, 4).

Many of the benefits and reasons for using CPS with students are similar to other problem-solving strategies. First and foremost, creative problem solving promotes higher-order thinking skills because the problems are open-ended. Students think both critically and creatively as they seek to find solutions to problems.

CPS gives students a reason to struggle a little bit. It keeps students from jumping rashly to solutions. The end result of completing something that was first perceived as difficult builds confidence for future challenging tasks.

The learning that takes place with CPS provides opportunities for students to work with others in collaborative groups. It prepares students to know how to work with others, which is valuable in the workplaces of today and tomorrow.

Finally, the strategies that students use in CPS will benefit them their entire lives. By using CPS, teachers are preparing their students for the workforce. Employers are looking for creative individuals whose ideas will make profits. Some of these students, with the proper training and encouragement, can go on to be the next great inventors of the time. CPS gives students the opportunity to build "creative muscles." The more one practices creativity, the more those creative muscles will grow.

CPS may still seem like a difficult strategy to implement in a classroom where standards are so important. Because of this, some teachers argue that they cannot implement CPS. However, Bronson and Merryman (2010) showcased a fifth-grade class that used CPS to investigate a problem. Teachers presented students with the problem of reducing noise in the school library, which had windows that faced a noisy, public space. Within this investigation, several key standards were met. They studied how sound traveled through materials and gained an understanding of sound waves. They learned per-unit calculations as they worked with various materials to find an inexpensive way to fund the project. And, they learned how to write persuasively. At the end of that year, scores on the standardized testing rose, placing their school in the top three in the city despite the fact that the poverty rate at this school was 42 percent.

Teachers can implement CPS by looking at key objectives from various content areas that need to be taught during the year. Then, they can form a problem that teaches this skill, concept, or generalization. At times, students will have ideas of real problems that they bring up in class discussions. Some great ideas for young students come from storybooks. Teachers can read through part of the book and stop when there is a problem presented. Then, place students according to their specific needs in small groups of no more than three students. They can be grouped heterogeneously, with teachers and parents monitoring all the groups and making sure that there is not just one student doing all the work, or they can be grouped homogeneously, where the below-grade-level students are heavily monitored. The English language learners should be dispersed among the homogeneous groups depending on their thinking abilities and where they feel most comfortable. Especially at the beginning stages of using CPS, students will need to be led through the steps of creative problem solving. This will need to take place over a period of several days. First, students must understand the problem. Next, students can generate ideas. Finally, students can make a plan for what they would do. Doing it in three distinct segments gives students time to think about solutions.

Finally, students can be assessed in both formative and summative ways. Students can write in their journals before they start the problem so that they are predicting. They can write during the problem solving so that their thinking process is shown. Finally, they should write after they have solved the problem to show how they came up with their final solution. Students can even produce a product like a persuasive letter or sign—the possibilities are endless.

Please note that teaching creativity is not the ultimate goal. The goal is to provide opportunities to *exercise* the creative muscles that are present in every student. Teachers can do this by resisting the natural inclination to be the answer provider. For every question a student asks, ask another question that makes that student look for answers. It can be as simple as *What do you think?* This takes practice and some getting used to. Do not worry if you do not know the answers. There is strength in admitting you do not know something. Students respect the honesty. We can, as adults, learn valuable things from our students. We are lifelong learners too, right?

The Wallas Model

Think of the times you have been jogging, in the shower, or just driving alone in your car. Suddenly, the answer to a problem pops into your head. You might not have been thinking about the problem at that moment, but mysteriously, an answer came to you. You were away from the problem for enough time for your subconscious to work it out. Even if your problem-solving process did not seem to go through a rigid set of steps, chances are you used what is known as the Wallas model.

In 1926, Graham Wallas outlined a set of four stages to creative problem solving in his book, *The Art of Thought*. In order, these stages are (1) preparation, (2) incubation, (3) illumination, and (4) verification. Most of the time, the steps will fall into this order. However, there are times that steps can be skipped or repeated as needed to find a suitable solution.

Preparation involves defining the problem. This is where every part of the problem is examined for full understanding and clarification. Relevant information can be gathered during this stage, including previous solutions to the problem that were not successful. Research materials can be collected in preparation for solving the problem.

The **incubation** stage is a reflection stage at which the idea sits for a while. Unconscious activity is taking place to help solve the problem. Some call this *fringe consciousness*, or *off-consciousness* or a *less-than-conscious* activity. Humans can only focus on one main activity at a time. Other activities can be done, but they are done at a lower consciousness. For example, you can type an email to a friend while also listening to music. However, listening to music is something that is done at a lower level of consciousness. You can walk, chew gum, and talk on your phone. But only one of these activities is the main focus. The problem-solving process works the same way. The problem can be worked out at a lower level of consciousness while another main-focus activity is going on. At times, the person can be doing something else completely unrelated to a problem he or she has been working on during the incubation stage. However, incubation can also be a time of reflecting on the problem. Teachers should encourage students to always carry a pad and pen with them to write down ideas as they come during the incubation stage. Having students leave the problem for a day or two can be a necessary step for this stage.

The third stage is the **illumination** stage. It is the *Aha!* moment. It is when the solution to the problem becomes clear. It usually comes suddenly on the tail end of days or even weeks of incubation.

Verification is the fourth and final stage of the process. It is characterized by checking to see if the solution is indeed the right solution to the problem. If the problem is not solved, then the other steps can be repeated until a good solution is found.

Perhaps the hardest part of the Wallas model is the incubation stage. This stage particularly can be a struggle for teachers who need to move through curriculum quickly. It takes time to allow ideas to come, and this can present problems in scheduling for teachers. However, it is a scheduling adjustment that is definitely worthwhile. Problem solving is a process that takes time. It is more important that students learn to struggle with a problem instead of expecting instant solutions, which are not always the best solutions. This prepares them for life outside school and for the future.

Teachers can use the Wallas model in all content-area classes:

- Mathematics teachers can present unfamiliar problems to students to see if they can figure out how to solve them.

- Social studies teachers can use the Wallas model while presenting diplomatic problems, mapping neighborhood issues, or assigning political campaign slogans and have students work to come up with ideas.

- Science teachers can use the model while having students invent a helpful gadget or come up with ideas for curing diseases.

- The Wallas model is helpful in language arts class as students work on titles for their creative writing pieces or need ideas for making speeches more interesting.

Decision-Making Strategies

We make decisions each and every day. Some of these decisions have big impacts on our lives, and other decisions have very little impact on our lives.

According to decision theorists, decision making is defined as the practice of making choices among contending courses of action (Raiffa 1968; Von Winterfeldt and Edwards 1986). They say that decision-making skills take problem solving one step further. As in problem solving, decision making involves evaluating possible courses of action. However, decision making must weigh conflicting objectives before deciding on a possible solution. And, decision making evaluates each course of action simultaneously. Decision making focuses on a clear goal or outcome.

Decision making skills should be taught to prepare students for the complex society we live in today. Today, there are so many more choices than there were for our parents and grandparents. Students need to learn how to navigate through choices so that they are prepared for adulthood. Learning decision-making skills can also help students overcome peer pressure. Learning to evaluate possible outcomes as a result of their actions might help steer them away from making harmful, life-altering decisions.

Such decision-making skills do not have to be limited to older students and adolescents. Young students can learn them, too. Begin by giving students a limited number of choices from which to choose. These choices may first be based on preferences (i.e., *Do you like this or that better?*), and then choices can become more complex. For example, teachers can provide students with frames of reference by asking them how other students who are affected by the choice might feel. Guide students to understand how their choices have consequences. As students grow older, this can be implemented even more. Lessons that include strategic-thinking activities, simulations, and games can be effective venues for teaching decision-making skills.

Strategic-Thinking Activities

Strategic-thinking activities help students prepare for success by organizing a plan in a thoughtful process. Learning how to think through a decision in a thoughtful manner can help them to avoid making rash decisions. It gives students the tools for becoming good decision makers as adults and in their careers.

Strategic-thinking activities naturally involve critical thinking, problem solving and, at times, teamwork. If specific steps were asssigned to strategic thinking, they would require students to do the following:

- Observe the situation

- Absorb necessary information

- Analyze the information

- Predict possible solutions

- Implement the idea

Being able to play chess involves strategic thinking and can be used at all levels between kindergarten through high school. Many types of mathematical games, video games, and board games today involve strategic thinking. The player's main goal is to outsmart his or her opponents and win. This type of thinking is not just for game playing, though. It is particularly helpful in organizations and businesses today. Employers train their employees to think strategically so that their company can move forward and succeed in their specific fields. Anyone who wants a promotion in a company must possess the leadership attribute of strategic thinking. Teachers can begin using strategic thinking by following a few basic steps.

1. Begin with a question. This question should be thought-provoking, e.g., *To solve this mathematical problem, we must . . . . To win the game, I must . . . .* Students can write down their ideas, or they can talk about their ideas with partners.

2. Let students share their ideas aloud. Make a short list of their ideas.

3. Continue to ask students *Why?* This helps them clarify their ideas and reason through them, sorting for the best possible game plan. The teacher serves as the guide to help students gain the understanding and objective of the lesson.

A few specific strategies to use within strategic-thinking activities that can help students reach goals are *decision trees*; *grid analysis*; and *plus, minus, interesting*. All of these are visual-support tools.

Decision Trees—This type of graph looks much like a tree where students can record the possible consequences or outcomes of a particular decision. It can help students see if the decision will reach the goal and determine whether it is worth the risk.

- To use a decision tree, students will begin listing a decision.

- After the decision is listed, two branches go in either a *yes* or a *no* direction.

- The consequences of the *yes* and the *no* are explained with two more branches, one off the *yes* and one off the *no*.

The figure below shows a template of a decision tree.

Fig. 5.2 Decision Tree Template

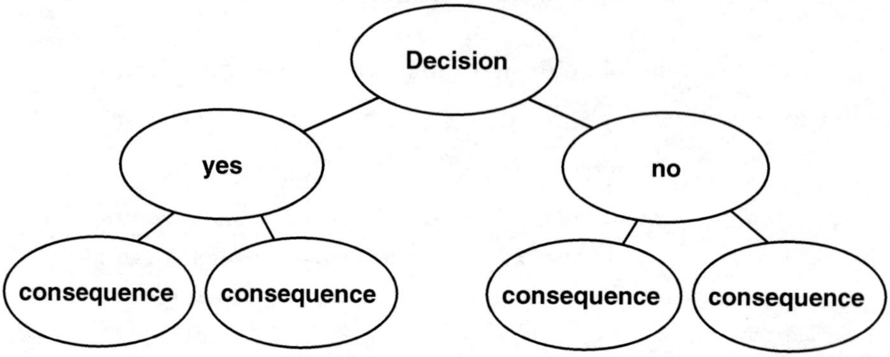

Grid Analysis—This graphic organizer acts as a three-pronged T-chart where students list all the possible outcomes along with the pros and cons of each decision.

- Begin by drawing a chart with three columns.

- One column should be reserved for listing the possible *outcomes*.

- Directly across each outcome should be listed the *pros* in the second column and the *cons* in the third column.

Students can then look at the three-column chart to see which outcome would be the most desired. All the pros and cons will be listed with each outcome so that students can decide which to select at a quick glance.

Plus, Minus, Interesting—Once students have listed the possible decisions they could make, they can rate each decision and outcome as plus, minus, or interesting (De Bono 1970). This can help them to eliminate choices much quicker. This strategy can take many different shapes and forms, such as the following:

- **Flower diagram**—Have students make three little flowers, with the center of the flowers being the plus (+), the minus (–), and the interesting (I). The notes about each one can be listed on each petal of the flower.

- **Graphic organizer**—Students can draw a pie with three sections. Each section will be either the plus (+), the minus (–), or the interesting (I). The notes about each one can be listed within each part of the graphic organizer.

- **Grid**—Make several three-column charts, one for each outcome, and have students list the pluses, minuses, and interesting things about each outcome.

No matter which visual strategy is used within the strategic-thinking activity, students can visually see the results of different decisions. These visual strategies help students to weigh consequences and can transfer to decision making, like deciding which car to buy, once they are adults.

Simulations

A simulation gives the appearance of a situation. It involves students experiencing a fictional situation in which they must make decisions that affect the outcome. When used properly, simulations can be powerful teaching tools that provide students the opportunity for decision-making situations. Since the situation is not real, mistakes involve very few repercussions. Students are free to take risks and learn from mistakes. Students realize that there are multiple ways to approach the situations. It also provides them a context for making decisions, and the learning experience can transfer to other situations in future decision-making opportunities. Simulations can be used as a way to introduce a topic, demonstrate important facts about a topic, or as a conclusion to show what students have learned.

Simulations and games are among the most effective teaching tools to help students learn how to make decisions. They increase the retention of content over time as opposed to traditional classroom instruction (Bredemeier and Greenblat 1981; Randel et al. 1992; Van Sickle 1986). Simulations increase student interest (Randel et al. 1992). When students are motivated and interested in the topic, they are more likely to learn. Through the use of simulations, students grasp the material better, too (Petranek 1994). The real goal in teaching is that students learn, and simulations are tools that bring about better learning. Even so, in no way should simulations be the only tool used for learning in a classroom. They should be used in conjunction with other teaching methods.

Simulations do demand upfront time from the teachers. Perhaps the lack of time to prepare deters some teachers from using simulations and games. For many, however, the results of these active learning strategies outweigh the commitment of preparation.

The generic steps of a simulation that involves decision-making strategies can be as follows:

1. First, students identify the need to make a decision. This can come from presenting a situation to students. This must have a hook or catch to make it interesting. There are many ways to hook students, and teachers should be creative when presenting a situation to their classes. For example, teachers can hang up posters announcing it, read a situation to students, or address letters for students to read.

2. Students then define the situation or issue at hand in their own words. Before they can make a decision, they need to understand fully what they are deciding and what the ultimate goal is. Depending on the simulation, this step can involve various amounts of research. It can also involve brainstorming possible solutions. For this step, students can be placed in small groups, or with partners, or they can work individually.

3. Students then evaluate and make judgments regarding what they need to do. Which course is the best to take? At times, students might want to make a grid of all their options, listing the pros and cons of each one. What are the expected results? This can help them to narrow their ideas down to the best option. Possible decision strategies to use with students can include same strategies mentioned in strategic-thinking activities:

Decision trees

- To use a decision tree, students will begin by listing a decision.

- After the decision is listed, two branches go in either a *yes* or a *no* direction.

- The consequences of the *yes* and the *no* are explained with two more branches, one off the yes and one off the no. (Figure 5.2 shows a template of a decision tree.)

Grid analysis

- Begin by drawing a chart with three columns.

- One column should be reserved for listing the possible *outcomes*.

- Directly across from each outcome should be listed the *pros* in the second column and the *cons* in the third column.

Plus, Minus, Interesting

- **Flower diagram**—Have students make three little flowers, with the center of the flowers being the plus (+), the minus (–), and the interesting (I). The notes about each one can be listed on each petal of the flower.

- **Graphic organizer**—Students can draw a pie with three sections. Each section will be either the plus (+), the minus (–), or the interesting (I). The notes about each one can be listed within each part of the graphic organizer.

- **Grid**—Make several three-column charts, one for each outcome, and have students list the pluses, minuses, and interesting things about each outcome.

4. Students make a plan of action next. They decide how they are going to implement their decision. They can make a time line of their decision to show exactly what they will be doing.

5. Students evaluate the results of their decisions and consider the following questions: Would they make any modifications for next time, and what did they learn through the activity? This is a great opportunity for assessment. Students can write their reflections or discuss them. Teachers can make checklists to keep track of student responses and reflections.

Games

Games are a fantastic way to motivate students. There are very few students who are not attracted to games. When teachers can use games that have the right amount of challenge, students can develop important decision-making strategies in a safe environment. The environment is safe because these games do not have any bearing on the real world. Whether they are board games, card games, or virtual games, students get to practice making decisions in a "real-world setting" without real-world repercussions and consequences. It is one way to present content and also vary the teaching method for other learning styles.

It is important to make a clear distinction between games meant for review and games that promote higher-order thinking. Many teachers use games to help students review key concepts that they need to learn for tests. These types of games do have value; however, they do not necessarily promote higher-order thinking.

Games that promote higher-order thinking have several characteristics. They require that students evaluate, create, or analyze. Students must think deeply instead of just looking for facts that answer questions. These games should cover new material or at least material that students have not had much exposure to previously. They involve some level of problem solving and should stimulate creative thinking. These games also help students apply their knowledge to new contexts.

Some computer games target higher-order thinking as they require students to make decisions that have virtual outcomes and consequences. One benefit of virtual games is that there are very little constraints like money or location. Students are naturally attracted to all kinds of computer games, from those in phone apps to home video-game consoles. When teachers can find educational games in these venues that teach or reinforce important standards, then they have found the best of both worlds.

When planning games that promote higher-order thinking, consider the following:

1. Decide the skills and objectives you want the games to teach.

2. Decide on a game that can teach these skills and objectives.

3. Decide on the goal of the game and consider the following questions: What are students striving for? How will they know when they achieve this goal?

4. Plan the rules that players must abide by to reach the goal. Decide whether students will compete against the clock, themselves, or other players.

5. Evaluate the created games to be sure that the activities in the games are challenging, but not too easy or too difficult. If students respond quickly without any thought, then the game is too easy. When students have to think about their next steps and the resulting consequences, they are intellectually engaged in making decisions. They should stretch their thinking and struggle a little bit. Critical thinking skills must be a crucial part of this.

Games do demand upfront time on the teacher's part unless there are ready-made games to use with students. However, the final results of using games are worth the time investment. When students are engaged and actively use higher-order thinking skills, they are more likely to remember the concepts and skills their teachers are trying to teach. The classroom will come alive with problem solvers, thinkers, and real application of concepts.

Idea-Generating Strategies and Activities

Brainstorming and Brainwriting

Perhaps the most widely used idea-generating tool is brainstorming. Brainstorming is a method of thinking up new concepts, ideas, or solutions. The basic idea is to generate as many ideas as possible within a time frame. If you have to choose, it is quantity over quality. The more ideas that are generated, the better the chance of finding a good solution. Many jobs and businesses depend on brainstorming to survive. New ideas are needed so companies can grow. Executives look to their employees to find answers. For these very reasons, brainstorming is an important tool for students to learn how to use. The more a person uses it, the better he or she will be at using it.

Brainstorming is a type of lateral thinking, as opposed to vertical thinking. Vertical thinking occurs when one solves a problem by going from one logical step to another (De Bono 1970). Lateral thinking comes from seeking solutions to problems through unconventional methods. Our brain is geared to recognize patterns and to follow a patterned way of thinking—also called vertical thinking. Practicing lateral thinking helps us break out of this habit so that we can generate new ideas.

Alex Osborn coined the term "brainstorming" back in 1939. Osborn believed that creative ideas should be expressed without any judgment or evaluation at first (Osborn 1993). Some of the ideas produced in brainstorming sessions will be wild and crazy, but often these ideas can lead to the best solutions. He believed it was easier to tone down a wild idea than to think up a completely new idea. Brainstorming is typically used in a group setting, but it can be used individually. First, ideas are shared and recorded without evaluation. Later, ideas can be evaluated.

Some general guidelines to follow are:

- Begin with an open-ended question for students to brainstorm. Share this ahead of time so students can begin thinking about the question.

- Assign a certain amount of time for the brainstorming session. Five to 15 minutes is a perfect amount of time.

- No one is allowed to criticize or judge ideas during the session.

- Encourage students to contribute ideas that are piggy-backed off other ideas. They do not have to be original.

- When the session is over, have students select the top three ideas. They should explain why they liked these ideas the best.

Another variation of brainstorming is reverse brainstorming, where the teacher lists the opposite of what is wanted. Some examples are:

- In what ways can this math problem be solved incorrectly?

- How can we increase the school's production of waste?

- What could the main character do to become more selfish?

- What makes a terrible leader?

In today's society, electronic brainstorming is a good alternative. Students can send in their ideas via emails, text messages, discussion boards, social networking sites, or Twitter™. With this, students can respond as soon as an idea sparks in their minds.

There are some people who disagree with the fundamental way brainstorming is used, saying that it is more useful individually than in large groups for generating good ideas. The first objection is that only one person can speak at a time. If a large group is present, many ideas could be passed up as participants eagerly wait their turn to speak. They also say that some people will not offer their ideas aloud because of fear of peer evaluation. Sharing aloud in a brainstorming session can magnify problems between two rival personalities. Regardless of which side you take, whether it is used individually or in group settings, brainstorming does have value for generating ideas.

Another form of brainstorming is *brainwriting*. The general rules for brainwriting are as follows:

1. Present the problem to students. Each student's paper can have a different question or problem, or they can all have the same question or problem.

2. Have students take one sheet of paper out along with something to write with. Each student will write down three ideas on their paper. Give students a three-minute time limit to write their ideas.

3. When the time is up, have students each pass their papers to the person on their left. Let students read the ideas on the new papers.

4. Provide students with three minutes to write their top three new ideas on the new papers. Ideas cannot be repeated; however, the ideas they just read can trigger new ideas to be written.

5. Repeat for a fixed number of rounds.

6. At the end of the lessons, consolidate the ideas and evaluate them for worth.

A combination of both brainstorming and brainwriting would be *carousel brainstorming*. Place students in small groups, with each group having a different-color marker. Have posters or papers distributed around the room with different open-ended questions on each one. Students carousel around the room, consulting with their group to write responses. They may not copy a response already written, but they may piggy-back off the ideas. Of course, this may be modified as an individual activity in which each student writes his or her responses.

The responsibility on the teacher's part is to model how to do it, monitor students as they produce ideas, and keep all negative comments at bay. When these are effectively done, brainstorming sessions are more likely to be productive.

Vocabulary activities such as listing antonyms, synonyms, definitions, and using the words in sentences are productive ways of using these types of brainstorming in the classroom.

This activity can extend into mathematics by having students take a measurement like 36 inches and convert it to other forms of measurement, like feet, meters, and centimeters. Or, students can list all the ways to make $2, such as 200 pennies, 20 dimes, 8 quarters, and a single $2 bill. Students can list the figures that are polygons and ones that are not polygons in the room.

In science, very young students can list all the things that magnets can move. Students in middle grades can list examples of where they see force and motion in everyday life. In the upper grades, students can focus on the different kinds of materials that respond to electric forces like insulators, semiconductors, conductors, and superconductors.

Students can list qualities of leaders or time periods in social studies class.

SCAMPER

Have you ever heard the saying, *"There's nothing new under the sun?"* Most ideas are modifications of something that already exists. SCAMPER, an acronym used for an idea checklist, is an adaptation of the 73 Idea-Spurring Questions created by Alex Osborn (1993). SCAMPER stimulates ideas and follows the notion that new ideas are modifications of something already in existence. SCAMPER helps students to think differently about their problem and challenge an idea to come up with unique ideas. Below, the acronym is explained.

SCAMPER	Defined	Questions to ask	Key words
Substitute	Is there a way to substitute something else for the product, process, or problem? Finding replacements can help you to find new ideas. Anything can be changed.	• Can I replace components? • Can I swap materials or ingredients? • Can I switch people? • Can I change the rules? • Is there another process I can use instead? • Can it be renamed?	• alternate • exchange • proxy • replacement • stand-in • surrogate • swap • switch
Combine	How can parts of the product, process, or problem be combined to create something entirely new or different? Combining unrelated items helps you to expand your creative thinking.	• Are there two parts of the problem that I could combine together? • Is there an unrelated component that I could integrate with this? • How can I combine materials? • What ideas can be merged? • Can I combine it with other objects? • How can I combine it with different talents to make it better?	• amalgamate • blend • bring together • come together • join • merge • mingle • mix • unite

SCAMPER	Defined	Questions to ask	Key words
Adapt	Can you find a similar solution or change to your problem that is already out there? Is there a way to borrow an idea and change it to make it your own?	• In what ways can this be altered? • How can I make this like something else? • What can I borrow or copy? • How can I change its function? • Is there a way to use part of another element? • How can this concept be adapted to another context?	• adjust • alter • amend • bend • change • fit • modify • revise • rework • vary
Magnify	How can this idea be exaggerated? By magnifying the situation, you can discover new insights about it as well as find out why it is so important.	• What can be made larger? • How can I increase it? • What can I do to exaggerate it? • How can I elaborate? • In what ways can it be made stronger? • How can I make it a bigger deal?	• amplify • attributes • blow up • elaborate • enlarge • expand • increase in scale • strengthen
Put to Another Use	How can your product, idea, or problem fulfill a different kind of need? At times, we can find effective uses for our ideas when we think of new ways they can be used.	• What else can I use this for? • How can this be used in an unusual way? • How would an animal use it? • How could a child use it? • How can this be used in a different context? • How could someone in a different country use it?	• apply • bring into play • employ • exercise • harness • make use of • operate • utilize

SCAMPER	Defined	Questions to ask	Key words
Eliminate/ Minify	How would eliminating or minimizing the problem, idea, or product change the situation? When we trim our ideas down to the bare necessities, we discover the most important parts of it.	• What can be made smaller? • How can I reduce it? • What can I do to minimize it? • In what ways can it be made weaker? • How can it be split into smaller parts? • How can this be understated?	• abolish • curtail • diminish • eradicate • minimize • lessen • reduce to core functionality • reduce in scale • remove elements • shrink • simplify
Reverse/ Rearrange	What would happen if the problem, idea, or situation were reversed or rearranged? Is there an unexpected benefit when it is done in a different order?	• How can I exchange components? • Can I switch the positives and negatives about it? • What would result if I made it go backward? • What would result if I did the opposite? • Can I rearrange it to make a pattern? • Can it be turned around? Down instead of up? Up instead of down?	• change • contrary • converse • invert • opposite • reorder • reorganize • repeal • reshuffle • swap • transpose • turn around

SCAMPER can work to help students broaden their understanding of book characters, events, people in history, and can also help in writing ideas. However, within certain content areas, SCAMPER, as described above, would be a difficult fit. For example, mathematical and scientific concepts might not need strategies that generate ideas. In these instances, SCAMPER is best used to broaden conceptual understanding of a topic or subject area. In mathematics, for instance, the SCAMPER activities example on the following page broadens students' conceptual understanding of a graph of a linear equation.

Mathematics example: Graph of the linear equation $y = 5x + 2$

Substitute: Change the slope to –5. What does this do to the graph of the line? (Answer: The line will change from a positive slope—rising from left to right—to a negative slope—falling from left to right.)

Combine: What other numbers and operations could be combined in this equation and still make it true? (Answer: Answers will vary. Students could perform the same operation on both sides of the equation and keep its integrity.)

Adapt: Square the variable x in the equation. What would this do to the equation? (Answer: Squaring the variable would change the linear function to a quadratic function.)

Magnify: Increase the slope by 5. What does this do to the graph of the line? (Answer: The line will become steeper.)

Put to another use: How can you use this function to show how something works in real life? Write a word problem to fit the function. (Answers will vary. Example: Gina is beginning a stamp collection. She already has 2 stamps. Each month, she purchases 5 more stamps. How many stamps will she have in x months?)

Eliminate/minify: Eliminate (subtract) the number 5 from the equation. What does this do to the graph of the line? (Answer: This would change the slope of the line to 0. The graph would change to a straight horizontal line at $y = 2$.)

Reverse/rearrange: Rewrite the equation as a variable expression equal to zero. (Answer: $0 = 5x - y + 2$)

Using SCAMPER in this way helps students understand the concept of line graphs. This could be adapted to the concepts of money and time for younger students and algebra and geometry for older students. In science, SCAMPER can be used to broaden students' conceptual knowledge of living things, particularly mammals.

Students can use the SCAMPER method in various ways. First, the problem, challenge, idea, or goal that you want to accomplish should be defined. Then, either sequentially work through the SCAMPER idea checklist to help generate ideas for a change, or skip around and use a few selected ones. Students can even place the words on different faces of a cube (combine two on one of the faces) and roll the cube. The one that lands on top must be worked on first. Then repeat the process for a specified amount of time or until all faces have been rolled. This offers a random way of going through SCAMPER and can increase the flow of creativity.

Thinking Organizers

Thinking organizers are tools that help us organize our thoughts in a visual manner. They can show how your thoughts about various concepts are connected. They can bring new meaning to a group of ideas or problems. Each student's thinking organizer will look different, because students think differently. It will represent how they think. Thinking organizers can be compared to graphic organizers, which are used quite frequently by students to record what they have learned about a topic. However, the difference between these two types of organizers is that graphic organizers tend to be more rigid and are primarily used for finding and recording information. Thinking organizers are more open ended and show specific patterns of thought about a particular problem, situation, or concept. For this very reason, thinking organizers are very individualistic.

Even though thinking organizers are individualistic, there are some steps to take when creating them:

1. Create some sort of organizational image. Begin by writing down thoughts in some sort of graphic organizer fashion, using circles, bubbles, squares, or any sort of shape.

2. Have students free-associate ideas related to that first idea. Arrows can show how one thought is connected to, or leads to, another thought. These thoughts do not have to be in complete sentences. In fact, it is better if words, images, or phrases are used. It should make sense to the person who created it. Ideas can always be added to the thinking organizers later.

3. As ideas are added to the thinking organizers, associations should be made between the ideas listed. If necessary, students can take the ideas listed and reorganize them under certain headings or groups.

When teachers model this exercise, they should point out that their thinking organizers might be different from what a student might create and even model how other maps might look. It might also be helpful to have other students demonstrate for the class how they create their own thinking organizers.

One benefit is that thinking organizers give teachers a glimpse into how his or her students think, which can be invaluable information. Because it is a personal activity, another benefit for using thinking organizers is that students can write down their ideas freely without fear of judgment from others. It also provides a venue for uninterrupted flow of thinking or free-association and encourages concentration on the idea at hand because it limits students to think about one thing. All other activities are blocked off, and the paper with the ideas is the final focus. Finally, thinking organizers can expand as needed when new ideas come to mind. At some point, a great idea will appear that can be acted upon.

Creative Strategies

Creative Dramatics

Creative dramatics is a form of imaginary play that does not use written dialogue. Students create their own actions and words to show what they know about something. It relies on the students' willingness to act out scenarios. It is often described as structured, goal-oriented play. For example, younger students might act out the life cycle of a butterfly, and older students might act out how molecules respond when they are cold or hot. When students act these out, the teacher can assess how well students know the content. It also reinforces the concepts for students who are participating and watching.

There are many strong arguments in favor of using creative dramatics. Creative dramatics fully utilizes higher-order thinking skills because students interpret, organize, and synthesize ideas (Block 1997; Cox 1983; Froese 1996; Harp 1988; Miller and Mason 1983). It involves active learning experiences by engaging and stimulating students' imagination (Block 1997; Kelner 1993). Researchers say that to understand their world, children use imagination and play as opposed to logic and reasoning, which is used by adults (Holt 1983; Wagner 1988; Wolf 1993). Creative dramatics uses play and imagination to help students process the world of reason (Froese 1996; Kelner 1993). Creative dramatics is also physical and emotional. When students are emotionally involved in learning experiences, they are more likely to learn and remember the concepts (Block 1997; Bolton 1979). Another benefit is that student comprehension of texts and understanding of material increases as a result of participating in activities that utilize creative dramatics (Block 1997; Harp 1988; Henderson and Shanker 1978; Miller and Mason 1983; Wagner 1988). Creative dramatics is a tool that promotes vocabulary and language growth, which is a need, considering the new language-learner populations in many countries today (Block 1997; Edwards 1997; Froese 1996; Heinig 1993; Kelner 1993).

Creative dramatics involves four basic elements (Johnson 1998):

1. **Structure**—At first, teachers need to model how they want the creative dramatics to look in their classroom. One way to add structure is by having younger students act out very short and specific dramas. This is a good rule of thumb while allowing older students to lengthen and broaden their dramas as time allows. Most students will need the structure of knowing where to begin with their dramas.

2. **Open-ended scenarios**—The "scripts" of creative dramatics should never be written down, but rather be open-ended and more of an improvisational activity. Students should learn how to find their own ways of imparting meaning to their dramas.

3. **Safe environment**—Students should feel safe in the classroom, so that they can express themselves in their dramas. Doing this sort of activity demands that students take risks, and it is best if the teacher can model this for students, thereby taking a risk, too.

4. **Feedback**—Teachers need to provide positive feedback to students after they perform, pointing out the good qualities of their dramas. When students receive positive feedback, they are more likely to participate again, which increases their confidence and creative abilities. Teachers can encourage other students in the class to offer positive feedback based on the elements of voice, how students use their bodies to act, characterization, and how well they work in groups.

To focus on the four elements of voice, how students use their bodies, characterization, and how well they work in groups, teachers can have students practice by using the following activities in isolation:

- **Voice**—Provide a sentence and have students say it using different emotions such as *painful, happy, surprised, nervous, angry,* or *jealous.* Teachers can take popular lines from stories, movies, commercials, or key vocabulary words and try this exercise. For example, "Are you going to eat that?"

- **How students use their bodies to act**—Have students act out various scenarious with an emphasis on how their body would move in this situation. Possible scenarios might include seeing a lion in the classroom, winning an award, acting like an ant at a picnic, walking like a bowl of gelatin, etc.

- **Characterization**—Have students act as if they were famous people, book characters, important scientists or mathematicians, historical figures, numbers in an equation, etc.

- **Group work**—Teachers can remind students to be on the lookout for others who work well in groups. Do they include ideas from others? Are they respectful? Do they get their work done?

While at first it may seem that creative dramatics would be better suited for younger students, some of these examples show that creative dramatics can be used effectively with students of all ages. Topics do not have to be silly but can be more serious in nature with older students. For example, many teachers use creative dramatics to teach social skills and values. What are appropriate ways to treat one another? It can be used for role-playing to reinforce something. It can also be used to show what happened during a time in history, how elements react to one another, or the results of mathematical expressions.

Creative Writing

Creative writing is a means by which students can express their thinking and ideas. It can give them the opportunity to experiment with language while also showing what they know and have learned about a topic. Creative writing is not just for language arts class. Teachers can effectively implement creative writing across all the content areas as a means of assessment.

There are many benefits to creative writing. First, it encourages creativity because it is an open-ended activity. Imaginations take over and students can infuse their ideas into their writing. Second, creative writing involves higher-order thinking. Most teachers assign research papers to students to show what they have learned after researching a topic. However, research papers are little more than regurgitating facts about a topic. That is not to say that writing research papers should be ignored, but there are ways to use creative writing as an alternative. Facts and knowledge can be infused into creative writing, but students must invent ways to do it. The lower-order thinking skills are involved in creative writing because students must understand the facts and concepts about a topic. However, the higher-order thinking skills are also employed because the topic has to be presented in a new and creative way. Third, creative writing provides the opportunity for both playful and rigorous use of language. The imaginative ideas must work within the piece being written. This takes careful skill and craft on the writer's part. Creative writing breaks up the monotony of how students must respond with what they know. Students can write fictitious dialogues, cartoons, stories, commercials, or talk-show scenes that tell important facts in creative ways. This is more engaging for both the students and teachers and, because of this, such activities will produce better results. Finally, being a strong writer is applicable in all subject areas (language arts, mathematics, science, social studies, physical education, and music) and all aspects of life.

Strength in written expression will serve students well outside school, both in the workplace and in discourse with the real world. For example, students might feel confident enough to write a short response to the newspaper either agreeing or disagreeing with an editorial. They might create arguments that change the management's mind for the ways something should be done at their places of work. They will possibly write coherent evaluations for employees.

The teacher's role is to model good writing for students, and he or she can do this in a few ways:

- Teachers must be reminded that excellent writers are not just born. Students can learn how to be effective writers, and this begins with modeling. Students need good examples from which to learn.

- Teachers can present short pieces from well-known authors for students to analyze and emulate.

- Teachers can also write pieces for their students to analyze. It takes a high amount of bravery and risk on the teacher's part to do this, but the payoff can be tremendous. Students will be more likely to take risks if they see their teachers doing it too. It also models that learning continues after the school years and that they will be lifelong learners, just like their teachers.

Most teachers feel comfortable assigning creative writing in language arts or reading classes, but creative writing can be very useful across the curriculum as well. The table on the following page demonstrates some ideas of how creative writing can occur throughout the different content areas.

Creative Writing in Content Areas

Content Area	Creative Writing Ideas
Mathematics	• Write a dialogue between numbers involved in an inequality that describes how they feel about it and why it is an inequality instead of an equation. • Draw an illustration that explains the differences between perimeter and area. • Write a set of instructions for how to find the area of a wall on which the students will hang wallpaper of their own design.
Science	• Write a song about the water cycle from a raindrop's perspective. • Write about the digestion system from the food particle's perspective.
Social Studies	• Write a speech as if you were the president elected after Lincoln's assassination telling about the climate of the struggling country. • Compose an interview with Gandhi that tells about his hunger strikes and how he hopes civil disobedience will work. • Become an important piece of geography and beg others to come and visit. Describe what they will observe when they get there.

Teachers can take these types of creative writing assignments and grade them for content knowledge. Teachers should use rubrics that specifically tell students what they need to include in their writings. And, as always, these rubrics should be explained to students before they begin their work so that they know how they will be graded.

Project-Based Learning

At its very core, project-based learning engages students with content while having them produce projects to show what they have learned. It is an avenue by which teachers can have students "do something" instead of "learn about something." Most importantly, project-based learning replaces those dull worksheets and utilizes higher-order thinking skills. However, just because a worksheet turns into a project does not mean that higher-order thinking skills are part of the process.

Some projects can be no better than assigning busy work. This typically happens when the lowest form of thinking is involved to produce the projects. According to Larmer and Mergendoller (2010), meaningful projects fit two criteria: the work must be personally meaningful and should fulfill an educational purpose. But, does just researching a topic and creating a display of some sort—Web page, yard sign, or postcard—ensure that the assignment taps into students' higher-order thinking skills? Not necessarily. Creating projects that tap into students' higher-order thinking takes purposeful planning.

Larmer and Mergendoller (2010) propose several key elements that every good project needs. The first is an engaging entry point to the topic. This experience can be a video, discussion, guest speaker, field trip, or scenario, just to name a few ideas. The goal is to get students to care about the topic and personally accept the challenge of the assignment. Second, there should be a driving question that frames the project. Examples might include concrete questions (*Do science fair projects help students understand science better?*), abstract questions (*When is it not right to tell the truth?*), or problem-solving questions (*What can we do to make math class more interesting?*). Whatever the question is, it should work toward the goal of what you want students to learn while doing their projects. Third, students should be given choices when it comes to working on projects. Giving students choices results in better work that is turned in. Project-based learning activities are perfect for this reason because they are learner-centered, giving students control over what they will be producing.

One benefit of project-based learning is that the time devoted to it can be very flexible. Teachers can decide the length of an activity. Will it take place over a long period of time or in a very short amount of time? To shorten the time frame, teachers need to offer project choices that can be completed quickly. For example, instead of the teacher assigning a wiki page, he or she can assign students to create a trading card. By assigning this activity, students have the opportunity to demonstrate what they know about a person, place, or thing that they have been studying while also adding in a component such as predicting what is coming next for that person, place, or thing.

When applicable to the projects, project-based learning can help to develop valuable research skills. Sometimes, teachers expect students to know how to research a topic, which is not always the case. When teachers select project-based learning activities, they are motivating students to learn how to research topics, expand on their knowledge, and create unique and creative products.

Project-based learning provides students with the opportunity to work in groups or individually. Working with others prepares students for the workplace that they will enter someday. Learning how to manage their time working alone will help them become more efficient workers. Both of these skills need to be practiced.

For most students, time management is a skill that needs to be learned. A strategy teachers can use is incorporating checkpoints to help students successfully complete projects on time. While the time frame for projects can vary, it is important to teach students how to successfully manage their assignments.

Project-based learning activities provide concrete assessment pieces because they show how students apply what they learn, and each one is in a unique creative format. One problem teachers face is how to assign grades to creative works. Typically, teachers grade on neatness, grammar, and timely completion because it is difficult to grade creative works. It is important to consider how students benefited from and what they learned by completing the assigned projects. The teacher can encourage students to explain their projects and offer grades according to what they see and what is explained to them. This method allows the teacher to assess if students gained knowledge by completing the projects.

To make the most of project-based learning, teachers should plan backward:

1. Decide on what you want students to learn.

2. Choose the driving question that will frame the projects.

3. Decide how much time should be devoted to this project. Will it be a little time (one class period) or a few weeks? For younger students, a shorter time frame is suggested.

4. Based on the outcome of Step 3, decide on the project selections that students can choose from. These projects should be completed within the time frame you allow. If the project is set for a longer time frame, set checkpoints to keep students on task and accountable for their work.

5. Use a spreadsheet or checklist to keep track of project checkpoints. If used effectively, project-based learning will train your students to manage their time, use their creativity, and learn important content.

Open-Ended Tasks

Remember the *Choose Your Own Adventure* series of books? Many of us enjoyed these books as children. We felt we were in control of the story, and in very small ways, we were. We could reread the story many times and choose different outcomes for the characters. These stories were open-ended in the sense that we had choices with several outcomes. However, to make these stories truly open-ended, the stories would end unresolved and the readers would have to write the endings. Open-ended means that the end result is crafted by the creator (in our case, the student). The end result is open, not closed. Unlike this beloved book series from our past, the possibilities in open-ended tasks are really endless.

Some teachers might worry about using open-ended tasks for various reasons. Assessment can be difficult when teachers cannot compare student behavior. To help, teachers must rely on rubrics to grade this sort of work. Teachers also worry about how much control they must give up when they offer open-ended tasks. However, giving up this control allows students to display their creativity, which lifts the ceiling of expectation. Teachers will never know exactly how creative a student can be until they offer open-ended tasks to see exactly what they are capable of doing. Many teachers are afraid that open-ended activities mean chaos in the classroom; however, careful planning on the teacher's part can prevent chaotic situations. In fact, open-ended tasks that reach real objectives require that teachers craft them carefully with an end result in mind. Finally, some teachers feel uneasy about planning tasks that are open-ended because they simply do not know how to do it. The good news is that teachers can learn how to do it and do it effectively. The more a teacher practices planning these activities, the better the tasks will become and the easier implementation will be.

Open-ended tasks should be used with students for the student creativity reason listed previously. These tasks also provide a break in the often routine nature of teaching and learning. Most students are used to an expected outcome, the right answer, or one-size-fits-all learning. Open-ended tasks change the learning environment and have the benefit of possessing the "excitement factor" because teachers do not know what is to come, how something could be resolved, or what could be created. There is no reason why some amount of structure cannot be applied to the task to limit the parameters for the desired outcomes, but in no way does this diminish the power of this strategy to produce creative results as well as an exciting learning experience.

Open-ended tasks work well in every content area. For example, in writing, teachers can have students create either nonfiction or fictional accounts about a specific topic. Story starters are also an excellent and easy way to implement open-ended tasks.

Open-ended questions can be used to assess reading comprehension. For a student to be able to answer a *what if?* question (which is one example of an open-ended question), he or she must know the content of the story and characters.

Open-ended tasks in mathematics can include having students create their own patterns, equations, graphs, and games that show what they know about a topic. In fact, open-ended tasks can offer a very true assessment of what students know. Students can correctly guess the answers on multiple-choice questions and worksheets, but creating their own representation of what they understand about a topic can provide a much clearer picture of what they know.

Most scientists today perform open-ended tasks. They choose the experiment, decide on the procedures necessary, and then interpret the results. While this may be too much to begin with in any given classroom, a teacher can slowly offer some openness in one of these steps. Students have to first know what to do, and this typically comes with modeling how to conduct experiments. Open-ended tasks in science could include recording data in any format that students desire to show what they learned from an experiment. Instead of writing a research report on DNA, students could create a story that contains real facts about DNA. Instead of giving the steps for an investigation, give students the question to investigate and have students create their own steps.

Social studies activities that are open-ended can help students to see different points of view as they create a variety of projects, questions, and procedures for understanding social studies content better. Teachers can write open-ended questions on posters and have students carousel around the room to answer the questions. This type of activity works well for covering controversial topics, opinions, and biases. Teachers can frame situations in history using the words *What if?* It can become a writing activity, a discussion, or a basis for projects.

Conclusion

Higher-order thinking is a natural effect of using open-ended tasks. There are many strategies that develop higher-order thinking skills in students. Teachers can use different kinds of questioning strategies such as the Revised Bloom's Taxonomy, the Williams model, the Socratic method, and Depth of Knowledge. Additionally, teachers can infuse higher-order thinking into teaching by following the problem-solving strategies such as the problem-based learning model, Wallas model, decision-making strategies, strategic-thinking activities, idea-generating strategies and activities, thinking organizers and creative strategies, project-based learning, and open-ended tasks. By using strategies, teachers can have the opportunity to infuse the curriculum while promoting higher-order thinking in students.

Let's Think and Discuss

1. What will be the first new strategy mentioned in this chapter that you will use?

2. How do you envision this new strategy working with your content and your students?

3. Which strategy do you think would be the most difficult to implement? What steps can you take to ensure success when you use it in the classroom?

Chapter 6

Management Techniques to Facilitate Higher-Order Thinking

How in the world can I keep track of groups when I have a hard-enough time keeping track of individual work?

When using cooperative groups, a few students end up doing all the work.

Grouping students is unfair.

All students should have to do the exact same work, even if some are more capable of doing more complex work.

Managing a classroom can be one of the most difficult things teachers face, especially new teachers. But even the most experienced teachers can use fresh ideas to make things run more efficiently. On the following pages, different kinds of management ideas are discussed to help teachers make using higher-order thinking in their classrooms all that it can be. Teachers can use curriculum compacting, anchor activities, cooperative learning, and varied grouping strategies to keep things fresh and to consistently challenge all their students.

Curriculum Compacting

Even some of the most challenging work that a teacher prepares for his or her class might not be enough to challenge above-grade-level students. This is where curriculum compacting can help in a classroom. Curriculum compacting is a method of shortening the curriculum so that exceptionally bright students can move through it quickly. This allows students to pursue other interests and more challenging activities. Curriculum compacting is designed to allow above-grade-level students to work through the curriculum at a faster pace. It is not really designed for students who are already familiar with or know the content knowledge that is being taught. Rather, these students still need to learn the content, but they can move much quicker than others.

Within any given higher-order thinking task, if students show that they need more challenge than what is provided, allow them to work on independent activities like learning contracts that are based on higher-order thinking tasks. These tasks must be meaningful and not merely busywork to keep these students engaged and motivated to learn. The idea is to make the activities on the learning contract meet all the standards but also be more in-depth. These students must be self-motivated learners who have an organizational system in place to help them keep track of their work and their time. Teachers will need to have a system for checking up on their work so that these students are not left without accountability. Checklists should be used as well as contracts to keep parents, students, and teachers on the same page and to ensure that students are learning. If students fail to meet the rules in the contract, they should return to the class activities and complete work with the rest of the class.

For example, a language arts class might be reading a novel in literature circles and having group discussions. Curriculum compacting could allow an above-grade-level student to read the novel independently and complete the most complex discussion questions in written form. When this student finishes, he or she could be assigned another challenging book to read and corresponding complex questions to complete. In essence, this student moves at a quicker pace and is ready to complete the challenging work. The easy questions have been omitted because they would be busywork for this student.

In a mathematics course, a teacher could decrease the number of problems an above-grade-level student would complete on an activity page, reserving only the most difficult problems for the student. If the student can complete the difficult problems, he or she can move on to the next activity page. There is no need to complete the easy problems if this student can do the most complex ones. In this way, the teacher has compacted the work for this student.

In science, a student might skip over certain experiments if he or she can show knowledge and a thorough comprehension of the topic. Experiments are created to introduce or reinforce these concepts. There is no need for this student to complete experiments that he or she already understands in depth. Instead, this student could do a more complex experiment or work on the next topic coming up, possibly performing an experiment for that new topic.

In a social studies class, students might be studying a set of primary source documents about the Civil War. To compact the curriculum, the teacher would ask only the most complex questions about a primary source document for above-grade-level students. The easier questions are not assigned to these students. Taking this approach respects the abilities of this student instead of making him or her do dull repetition work solely for the sake of completing all the work.

Anchor Activities

Inevitably, there will be times that students finish their work early. This does not necessarily mean that the assignment was lacking in rigor. Some students might have worked really hard and, as a result, finished much earlier than the rest of the class. In these situations, it is important to plan structured activities for these students. If not given something to do, early finishers may disrupt the rest of the class.

Anchor activities are great venues for using higher-order thinking. Anchor activities are rigorous assignments that students complete when they have finished the class assignment. They can tie in to the main concepts being taught in class to not only reinforce the concepts but also expand them so that students think about them at higher levels. Or, they can be used as isolated practice activities for higher-order thinking. Teachers can also use anchor activities first thing in the morning. Students who arrive early can work on these activities before class begins. Students wanting to take home a challenging activity can complete these as extra-credit assignments. In any case, they should be engaging and fun.

Often, the purpose of anchor activities can be confusing or unclear to teachers. They mistakenly plan activities that prove to be busywork for the students who finish their work early. A busywork approach implies that these activities involve very little thinking. However, the students who finish quickly and have done their work well are the last ones who need busywork or work that merely reinforces the concepts. And often these students learn to not be so "smart" because it means that they will only have more work to do, since their "reward" for working hard is more work, this can lead to some students becoming underachievers. However, if anchor activities are planned correctly, they can engage students with higher-order thinking and push them to think more deeply about concepts. In doing so, anchor activities can be a great differentiation tool for these learners.

There are two basic reasons why anchor activities may sometimes be used ineffectively in the classroom. The first reason is that teachers do not know how to plan these types of activities to exemplify higher-order thinking skills. Second, teachers often feel they do not have the time to adequately plan these activities. This boils down to realistically doing what they can for students. Some teachers feel paralyzed by the amount of work they need to put into preparation of these types of extra activities. However, with some manageable strategies under one's belt, any teacher can prepare effective anchor activities. First, teachers need to know how to create them. Anchor activities can be designed using the strategies in this book. Keep in mind that the main goal is to engage thinking.

Sample anchor activities can include ongoing projects, simple one-page activities, or anything in between. Following are some ideas for anchor activities in the specific content areas. The main keys are to make them both challenging and engaging.

Language Arts

In a language arts class, teachers can use various engaging writing prompts that target characterization (or any specific skill) and have students write a storybook that can be shared with other younger classes. One example of this might be a "*What If*" book. This type of story engages the imagination and creativity and uses higher-order thinking skills. Or, students can create new and unusual characters by combining two characters they have studied, either visually in drawings or in written descriptions.

Mathematics

In mathematics class, an anchor activity assignment might have students prepare mini-lessons that teach a topic relevant to the class. The teacher can then allow students to teach the lesson either to the class or to another class. For example, if the topic of study is patterns, teachers can introduce Fibonacci numbers in the anchor activity. If the topic is measurement, students can list all the unusual things that can be measured in the principal's office.

Science

In science class, anchor activities might include various experiments. To act like real scientists, students should design experiments that test the things they wonder about. The teacher can provide students with examples of how a question can turn into an experiment. Then, students can be challenged to do the same with a few provided testable questions. Once students learn how to do this with the provided questions, they can offer their own questions and design experiments around those. Doing this type of activity not only includes higher-order thinking but also demonstrates the real way that scientists act.

Social Studies

In social studies class, anchor activities can include *if only* scenarios created by the students to show how any particular historical time period could change *if only* different kinds of decisions had been made or *if only* different leaders had been in power. Students must speculate on how things would be different based on what they understand and know about the time periods, decisions, and leaders. All of this involves higher-order thinking and allows students to apply what they know to be creative.

Cooperative Learning

It will not be too long before our students enter the real world and take on jobs that our parents could never have imagined would be possible. These jobs will require that students process information efficiently and collaborate with others to meet the needs of this ever-changing global society. Learning to work collaboratively with others is a skill. Some colleagues are difficult to work with. Teachers cannot just expect that when students become adults, they will be able to successfully work with others. Like anything else, students will need some preparation to be successful as team players. Providing opportunities that involve cooperative learning is one method teachers can use to prepare students for their future environments.

Cooperative learning is generally defined as teams of students working together to learn academic content. Cooperative learning has several benefits. Students who learn in cooperative environments show improved self-concept, positive interaction with peers, and positive outlook toward their peers (Johnson and Johnson 1999). Cooperative learning improves social skills as students learn to work with others and support one another in the learning process. Students are not only responsible for their own learning but are also responsible for their team's learning. In these teams, they form a supportive community as they help one another learn the content. Cooperative learning also helps students come to a deeper understanding of a topic (Barron 2008). Studies show that students who have worked in groups perform better on tests than those who have not worked in groups, gaining 28 percentiles in student achievement (Marzano, Pickering, and Pollock 2001). In fact, research shows that cooperative groups have especially benefited low-income students, minority students, and urban students both academically and socially (Barron 2008).

Cooperative learning should be both manageable for the teacher and beneficial for the students. To get the most out of cooperative learning, careful planning must take place.

First, teachers need to think about how they will assess individual student understanding of the concepts that the learning experience is designed to provide. This not only tells the teacher if specific students are not grasping the desired concepts, but also tells him or her if the learning experience is successful for everyone. Teachers can make adjustments to the activities to make sure students are learning key concepts, as well as take struggling students aside and work with them on specific content that is proving to be difficult. Students can then be assessed through quizzes, journal reflections, small projects, or tickets-out-the-door.

Second, teachers must make sure that all students are participating in the cooperative groups. There must be accountability. Too often, teachers have seen group work where one student does all the work. To make sure that this does not happen, all students need meaningful tasks that are equally proportioned. At the end of each task, students in groups can write individual sentences saying what they contributed to their group work. Everyone in the group should sign these pages. This serves as a peer assessment and provides students a way to be honest, making sure all students are pulling their weight in groups.

Third, teachers should provide rich learning activities for students to complete in these groups. Simply researching a topic and finding a way to report what students learn is not a higher-order thinking task. Higher-order thinking tasks require that students think deeply about something, analyzing, synthesizing, and evaluating it. Cooperative groups make great discussion groups. Teachers can ask questions that involve higher-order thinking and have these groups discuss it. Then groups can work together to produce products that challenge their thinking skills and work through problems to find viable solutions.

If used systematically and with structure, cooperative groups can be beneficial for student learning. The following section talks about how to group students for success.

Grouping

Research has shown that when students learn in groups (as opposed to working alone), they perform better (Lou et al. 1996). There are different ways of grouping students, and there are many variables a teacher must consider when grouping students to create a successful learning environment. These variables include gender, chemistry between students, social maturity, academic readiness, and special needs. Some students will work well together, while others will have great difficulty.

It is not necessary for teachers to name each group. However, if they do, they should try to change the names for leveled groups from time to time. For example, a teacher might use colors, animal names, or athletic team names to group students. One specific example of this is for a teacher to cut out and distribute three different colors of construction paper squares, with each color representing a different readiness level. The teacher would tell all the "yellow square" students to find partners who also have a yellow square. This way, the teacher creates homogeneous groups while also allowing students to choose partners.

The following grouping strategies demonstrate various ways to group students in a classroom.

Flexible Grouping

Flexible grouping is a strategy in which members of a group change frequently. More often than not, routinely using the same grouping technique can lead to negative feelings of shame or a stigma associated with some group levels, lack of appropriate instruction, boredom, and behavior problems in the classroom. Flexible grouping can change the classroom environment daily, making it more interesting. It takes away the negative feelings and stigma of the struggling students because groups are always changing. No longer are the struggling students always in the same group.

Flexible grouping can occur within the time frame of one lesson or over an entire unit. Try to modify groups from day to day, week to week, or unit to unit. Flexible grouping can include partner work, cooperative grouping, and whole-class grouping. Students' academic levels, interests, social chemistry, gender, or special needs can determine their placement in a particular group. Organization charts like the ones shown in Figures 6.1 and 6.2 can help the teacher keep track of how he or she is grouping students.

Homogeneous Grouping

Homogeneous grouping brings together students who have the same readiness levels. It makes sense to group students homogeneously for reading groups and for language and mathematics skills lessons.

To form groups, assess students to determine their readiness levels in a content area. Then, order students from highest to lowest in readiness and place them in order on a three-row horizontal grid.

One way to create homogeneous groups is by dividing students according to the chart below. Notice that students in the same row have similar readiness levels.

Fig. 6.1 Homogeneous Grouping

▲ Student 1	▲ Student 2	▲ Student 3	▲ Student 4
■ Student 5	■ Student 6	■ Student 7	■ Student 8
● Student 9	● Student 10	● Student 11	● Student 12

Heterogeneous Grouping

Heterogeneous grouping combines students with varied academic readiness levels. When grouping heterogeneously, look for some diversity in readiness and achievement levels so that students can support one another as they learn together.

Fig. 6.2 Heterogeneous Grouping

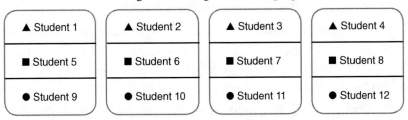

Another strategy for heterogeneous grouping is to group by interest. Interest groups combine students with varied levels of achievement to create groups that have common interests. Other strategies for heterogeneous grouping include allowing students to self-select their groups, grouping by locality of seating arrangements in the classroom, and selecting groups at random.

Flexogeneous Grouping

Flexogeneous grouping allows for the flexible grouping of homogeneous and heterogeneous groups within the same lesson. It involves the students switching groups at least one time to create another group during the lesson. For example, the homogeneous groups meet for half the lesson, and then switch to form heterogeneous groups for the rest of the lesson.

One easy flexogeneous grouping strategy is to jigsaw or mix up already established homogeneous groups. To jigsaw groups, allow homogeneous groups of students to work together for part of the lesson (circle, square, and triangle groups). Then, distinguish group members by labeling them A, B, and C within the same group. All the As form a new group, the Bs form a new group, and the Cs form a new group. In effect, the students from each group are combined with new members to form new heterogeneous groups.

Conclusion

Using the strategies mentioned in this chapter can help teachers manage the higher-order thinking classroom successfully. For students who learn more quickly, teachers can compact the curriculum through the use of learning contracts and assignments that allow these students to delve deeper. Anchor activities can be implemented for those who finish a task early. These activities should be grounded in higher-order thinking tasks instead of mere busywork. Teachers can utilize cooperative groups to give students practice working with others. Finally, flexible grouping should take place in any classroom that incorporates grouping techniques.

Let's Think and Discuss

1. Of the management techniques mentioned in this chapter, which will be the most beneficial for your classroom?

2. How can you integrate the management strategies discussed in this chapter with the strategies you already have in place in your classroom?

3. How will you plan on using flexible grouping in your classroom?

Chapter 7

Differentiating Higher-Order Thinking

> Differentiated curriculum and higher-order thinking are the same thing.

> When a teacher needs to differentiate, it makes sense to have just the above-grade-level students complete the higher-order thinking tasks.

> What if my below-grade-level students can't think on higher levels?

Different readiness levels, learning styles, and interests necessitate differentiated curriculum if *all* students are to advance their knowledge base. Many teachers differentiate curriculum by assigning higher-order thinking activities to higher-performing students and lower-order thinking activities to lower-performing students. And at times, this is appropriate. However, it does not have to be the hard-and-fast rule. Below-grade-level students need opportunities to think critically and creatively. They are capable of doing this, too. So, how can a teacher differentiate a higher-order thinking activity? This can be done in many ways.

Differentiating by Process

One way higher-order thinking activities can be differentiated is by process. In other words, the differentiation targets how the students will work on their assignments. It can be as simple as assigning different grouping techniques to support students. If all students have the same higher-order thinking task, a teacher can have the above-grade-level students work individually, the on-grade-level students work with partners, and the below-grade-level students work in a small group with the teacher. This grouping technique provides the needed support to complete the higher-order thinking task. The figure below shows what this representation looks like.

Fig. 7.1 Assigning Different Grouping Techniques

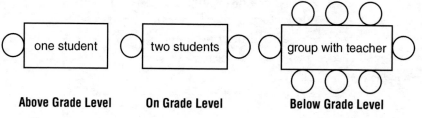

Each class will have specific needs because each student is unique. Depending on these specific needs, students can be grouped accordingly so that they can complete the higher-order thinking tasks successfully. For example, if a teacher knows that certain students will struggle with the higher-order thinking activity, those students should be grouped with other students who work well together and who could use the extra support. The right way to do this depends on the needs of the particular classroom, and the teacher knows those needs better than anyone else.

Another way to differentiate by process would be to differentiate the resources students are allowed to use while completing their higher-order thinking tasks. For example, struggling students might be given two or three teacher-selected books to use for information as they work on their tasks. On-grade-level students might be allowed to use two different teacher-selected informational websites to help them as they work on their tasks. Above-grade-level students might use a newspaper article tied to the topic to gain information as they work on their tasks.

It might take struggling students more time to process the content than it will take other students in the class. Assignments that are all tied to the same higher-order thinking skill may be differentiated by the amount of time students are given to complete it. Depending on the time constraints in a classroom, a teacher can work in small groups with struggling students to reinforce a concept and allow the other students to complete anchor activities or start in class and then assign it as homework.

Working with students who struggle academically will require more scaffolding. A teacher can present higher-order thinking tasks to them along with the entire class, but more support might be needed at times. For example, as students work on activity sheets based on higher-order thinking tasks, the teacher can provide support to the struggling students by giving them more information so that they can successfully complete the activity and learn the content. In a class studying a political cartoon, the teacher can ask everyone to answer the higher-order thinking questions but can also nonchalantly hand out clues on small pieces of paper or index cards to those who particularly struggle with the content. In this way, the teacher is not making a big deal about students needing extra support. Teachers can also provide more support to students by distributing leveled texts in place of the standard textbook text, which is often above grade-level reading. All students can participate in the discussion, which could be infused with higher-order thinking questions, but they will read the content at their readiness levels.

Some teachers complain that they cannot do the "song and dance" that they feel is required to address all the learning styles in their classrooms. By this, they mean teach the same lesson in several ways so that all their students can "get it." For example, a teacher may use Howard Gardner's Multiple Intelligences theory and try to teach a lesson incorporating all of the different intelligences. The motives of this teacher are good because he or she wants to reach all the students, but the fact of the matter is that teachers do not have the time to incorporate all the multiple intelligences into one lesson. A class period might only be 40 minutes long, and it would be near impossible and a real waste of time to teach that way. And, teachers do not have the time to plan every lesson this way. The idea is to be *efficient* in a classroom because teachers have to cover so much content.

Differentiating by Content

Teachers can cover a lot of material while differentiating curriculum and using higher-order thinking skills by differentiating the content. There are ways to do this and to get *all* students on the same page, content-wise, so that they can pass the tests. There will usually be students who are going to grasp certain content more quickly and easily than other content. Some content is tougher to master than other content because it might be more abstract or difficult to access. To differentiate in this way, a teacher can assign different content to groups of students. Everyone might have the same higher-order thinking questions or tasks to complete, but the content is differentiated according to readiness levels. It might look like the following:

- Above-grade-level students will tackle content that is more difficult.

- On-grade-level students will work on content that is challenging to them.

- Below-grade-level students will focus on content that everyone in the class needs to learn, but this content might be easier to access or "digest."

The figure below shows what this representation looks like. The important concept to keep in mind is that all students have the same higher-order thinking task.

Fig. 7.2 Differentiating the Content

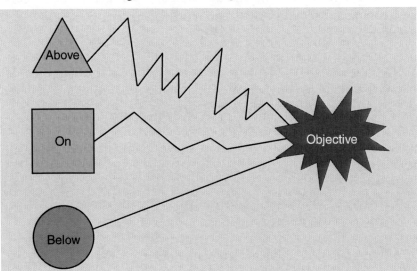

The teacher gives each group their content to learn either by researching it, reading about it and filling in a graphic organizer to record what they are learning, or answering questions about it. There are many activities a teacher can assign students while learning their specific content. The key is to offer higher-order thinking activities to all students while they are working on their specific content. Once students have completed their assignments, the teacher jigsaws—or mixes up—students. The students share what they know about their content in these new groups. All the different content should be represented in each group so that all students can benefit from learning all the content that is necessary. While learning the new content, a teacher can have students take notes, fill in graphic organizers, or have a set of higher-order thinking questions that students need to complete to make sure they learned the new content. The teacher can bring the class back together and ask pointed questions to make sure they learned all the content. Or, he or she could give a quiz or have students complete a ticket-out-the-door. An added benefit is that *all* students feel valued, even the below-grade-level students, because they had something important to share that the other students needed to learn. Another benefit is that the teacher has covered a large amount of content in a compacted amount of time. And finally, all students have completed activities that required them to think critically and creatively.

An example of tiered content in mathematics class might be as follows: Students can be given the same higher-order thinking activity, e.g., *Based on what you know about your topic, would you pay money to enter a contest based on the probability of winning?* Students would be provided with information and must show their concepts, which are tiered, below:

- Below-grade-level students studying how the concept of percents can be used to represent probability

- On-grade-level students studying how the concept of fractions can be used to represent probability

- Above-grade-level students studying how the concept of the word *odd* can be used to represent probability

The content for each of these groups is tiered according to the complexity of the content. However, all students need to understand all three of these concepts. The teacher can assign one higher-order thinking task to all the students, such as an evaluation question that they must explain to the other students when they are placed in heterogeneous groups.

A social studies example lesson would involve students studying about slavery through different leveled primary sources. Everyone is asked the same questions (e.g., *What was the creator's purpose in making this primary source? What does this say about that time in history?*) based on higher-order thinking, but students analyze different materials or content. In this example, the above-grade-level students are analyzing a runaway slave poster that demands they read between the lines to know what is really going on. The on-grade-level students have a poster that challenges their thinking. The below-grade-level students read a picture created by abolitionists and explain its meaning. Once students have studied their posters, the teacher can jigsaw the groups and have them share what they studied in new groups so that everyone gets the benefit of all three primary sources relating to slavery. Students can fill out graphic organizers or take notes as each student shares what they studied. This helps all students, especially the below-grade-level students, to feel valued because they have something important to share that others need to learn. As an added benefit, the teacher has been able to cover a lot of content in a shorter amount of time.

Fig. 7.3 Social Studies Example—Jigsawed Groups Tiered Content

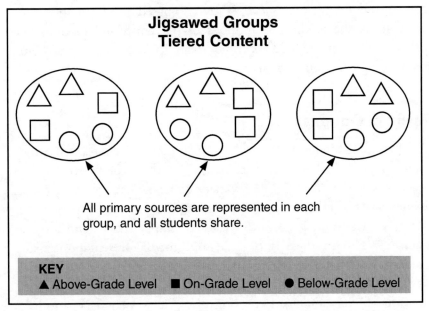

Differentiating by Product

Teachers can also differentiate higher-order thinking tasks by product. Students will have tiered products that they must complete, but all products are based on higher-order thinking. For example, if the concept is that students understand the predictable motions of Earth and the moon, the assignments could be as follows:

- Below-grade-level students will complete a set of four postcards that tell what would result if these motions were interrupted.

- On-grade-level students will complete newspaper stories that describe the havoc created as a result of these motions being interrupted.

- Above-grade-level students will complete text for a press conference that tells what citizens need to prepare for in affected areas because of these motions being interrupted.

The basis of this assignment is steeped in higher-order thinking by having students create a "*what if*" scenario based on information they learn about the predictable motions of the Earth and moon. The products are differentiated according to ability levels, with some being more complex and others simplified.

Menu of Options

Teachers can differentiate by allowing students to choose what they want to produce based on preference. In this type of situation, a teacher would want to offer a variety of tasks that are centered on higher-order thinking skills that are equally as challenging. For example, if one choice was to make a bumper sticker and another choice was to produce a 10-slide multimedia presentation, many students might choose the bumper sticker because it does not require as much work. Each project choice should weigh equally in the amount of work students have to invest. A better choice of products that require equal amounts of work would be as follows:

Civil War Battle of Gettysburg

Choices:

- Create a filmstrip of six slides showing the major events at Gettysburg.

- Use a map of the battlefield and show three major troop movements, one based on each day of the battle (July 1–3).

- Write three one-page journal entries that tell about the battle, one entry for each day of the battle (July 1–3).

Another way is to differentiate the questions by creating a hierarchy even among higher-order thinking questions. So, all students would be given the same content and process, but the questions would be different kinds of higher-order thinking questions. For example:

- Analyzing questions for below-grade-level students

- Evaluating questions for on-grade-level students

- Creating questions for above-grade-level students

Leveled Learning Centers

Teachers could also use these ideas in leveled learning centers where the activities or questions are leveled or tiered according to academic abilities, but still are all based on higher-order thinking tasks. Providing at least three leveled learning centers in a classroom will allow students to choose the center they would like to work in but will also give them an activity that appropriately challenges them. Within each center, there are activities that are appropriate for below-grade-level students, on-grade-level students, and above-grade-level students.

Activities can be modified for language to meet the needs of language learners. Using leveled learning centers provides busy teachers with time to assess students. As students work in their centers, teachers can observe students' checklists. So, if a student needs a more challenging task or more scaffolded work, assignments can be easily adjusted.

Choices Boards

Teachers can create choices boards with various tiered higher-order thinking tasks. Choices boards provide students with the opportunity to choose a few activities on a page, but the difficulty levels of the activities vary. It is similar to having several tiered assignments on one page. Each assignment could be a leveled higher-order thinking question or activity. A typical choices board could have 9 to 16 leveled activities on it. Three or four of the activities would focus on each type of learner: above-grade-level (triangle), on-grade-level (square), and below-grade-level (circle) students. In this example, a shape represents each academic level. Teachers can tell each student to choose two activities from the choices board that match the shape that the teacher assigns the student. For example, a below-grade-level student will choose two circle activities to complete. The teacher can tell that student to challenge himself or herself by choosing one square activity. There is not one hard-and-fast rule. The directions and design of these choices boards can vary as the student need varies.

Conclusion

Differentiating curriculum in a classroom does not mean that some students get to do higher-order thinking tasks and others need to do lower-order thinking tasks. There are specific ways teachers can differentiate while having all students think on higher levels. Even within higher-order thinking, there are levels of difficulty. Teachers can differentiate in the types of higher-order questions, tasks, or activities students complete. Teachers can differentiate by the process of how students learn, primarily involving different grouping strategies. Teachers can differentiate the content that students learn but still have all students completing higher-order thinking tasks.

Let's Think and Discuss

1. How are you already differentiating instruction for your students?

2. Of all the ways to differentiate described in this chapter, which one will be the easiest for you to implement?

3. What are some other ways you will be able to differentiate using higher-order thinking?

Chapter 8

Higher-Order Thinking for English Language Learners

What do I do with those English language learners?

They make us go back to basics, boring the rest of the class.

I can only ask lower level questions with English language learners.

It's like teaching a class within a class.

How can we challenge them without overwhelming them?

English language learners can't think critically.

Saved by Common Sense

When I first taught a class of English language learners, I had no idea what I was doing. I only knew that my class would have intermediate students that had taken an English class for two or three years in school. They knew *some* English. I never took undergraduate or graduate courses to learn how to teach English language learners. So, I turned to the only thing I had to help me conduct this class: common sense. I tried to imagine myself in their shoes. What would help *me* learn another language? I was expected to teach reading, writing, and conversation. I knew that everything we did needed to be meaningful to them.

My former students had always preferred books to abbreviated stories found in basal readers. So, I decided that these students should read a book instead of short stories or articles. I also knew students at this age had a love for fantasy literature and for J.R.R. Tolkien. I chose *The Hobbit*, a daunting book even for native English students. I found a dramatic audio recording of the book, purchased copies of the book for all my students, and created activity sheets that would encourage them to think both critically and creatively. Many of the responses were open-ended. I have to admit, I wondered if these students would be capable of doing them. During the class, I implemented various strategies for reading. I read aloud to them. We listened to the audio as we followed along in the book. The students read chorally.

I modeled strong writing techniques by bringing in a picture of my house. I asked them to give me a sentence about my house. I wrote it on the board. It was a very simple sentence. Then, I modeled how to change this simple sentence into a rich sentence by talking about adjectives and active verbs. They offered some that they knew, and I introduced new ones to them. The sentence transformed right before their eyes. These students applied this to their written responses about the book.

By the end of the course, the students remarked how they could not believe they had read an entire book in English. Their confidence soared, their writing skills improved, and their conversation was clearer (even though it had a little bit of my Texan twang to it).

Looking back now, it is amazing to me that I did all the right things. And, I saw that my students grow in their language acquisition. It was a very rewarding experience for me, and I learned two valuable lessons: (1) When given the necessary tools, English language learners are capable of higher-order thinking; and (2) Teacher expectations affect student achievement. I went into my class expecting that my students would read *The Hobbit*, and I provided support in every way that I could think of so that they could read it for understanding. Imagine the outcome if I only expected the three smartest in the class to read it? Only three would have succeeded, and I would have been satisfied with my expectations. Instead, I set the goal high for my students and they all met it. But, high teacher expectations are not enough. Along with expectations must come *action*. I needed to do whatever I could so that my students would be successful. Call it whatever you want: differentiate, accommodate, modify, etc. We must make the information accessible for students so they can learn it.

English Language Learners in Our Classrooms

The thought of teaching English language learners is an intimidating task for some teachers today. Like it or not, it is a growing reality for many school districts. Families move from country to country for various reasons. Suddenly, there is a diverse classroom. Teachers are already thrust into classrooms where they must teach to all levels of academic ability. To add another layer of complexity, English language learners are now included in the mix, and these learners are all at different levels of academic and language abilities, too. Many teachers feel overwhelmed because they do not know how to prepare for it. So, they decide to teach to the middle students or the low students. In many cases, this means omitting those higher-order thinking skills.

Is it possible to use higher-order thinking with English language learners?

Those who have traveled to other countries where English is not the official language find themselves understanding how some English language learners feel in our classrooms. I have traveled to small towns in Portugal, Israel, and Italy where no one speaks or understands English. How did I order my food? I pointed to what I wanted. How did I pay for it? That's a little scarier . . . I held out money in my hand and they took the amount. I found ways to communicate even though I had not acquired the language. It would be wrong of these people to assume that because I could not speak their language, I was incapable of higher-order thinking. If I had the necessary language tools (like sentence starters or vocabulary), I could tell them what I thought of their food and whether I would recommend it to other travelers. I could even write a review on my entire experience dining there, which would involve analyzing, creating, and evaluating.

Just because English language learners cannot express their thoughts in English does not mean that they lack critical and creative thinking skills. For these learners, the problem is language acquisition, not a cognitive disability. Every learner brings his or her cognitive abilities to a task. Researcher Jim Cummins states that conceptual knowledge developed in one language helps with making the input in the other language comprehensible (2000). Students who understand the concept of "migration" in their own languages only need to acquire the label for this term in English. Teachers can access that content knowledge by "tapping into background knowledge, scaffolding, and providing opportunities for students to transfer their knowledge into English" (Dong 2006, 10).

Research has shown that English language learners need to develop higher-order thinking skills alongside literacy and language skills (Cummins 1994; Dong 2004; Genesee 1994). According to Yu Ren Dong, "Learning a language is closely connected to learning to think critically in specific subject matter. . . By tailoring instruction to students' needs and meaningfully linking cognitive and linguistic elements in the learning process, teachers can help English language learners develop the higher-order thinking skills they need" (2006, 10). The author cites an example where an English language learner practices forming sentences in English. His teacher asks him very simple sentences, and the student responds with simple sentences, one of which does not make sense. He points out that the focus on sentence formation alone removes the learner from having to think deeply. Practicing sentences for the sake of just forming a sentence removes the learner from having to apply meaning. In these cases, the learner does not have to use higher-order thinking skills. To be effective, Dong stresses that instruction must integrate both thinking skills and literacy.

Ways to Integrate Thinking Skills and Language Development

Nothing can replace good teaching. If teachers were not so bogged down with paperwork, they could give their complete attention to teaching and doing it well. Not that documentation does not have its place and is not important—it is very important. But, somehow we have got to get back to doing what we know as best-teaching practices. Teachers should feel confident that these practices and strategies work well for all students, especially English language learners. In the same way that some might argue that what is good for gifted students is good for everyone, I would argue that some alternative strategies used to elicit responses from English language learners could benefit all learners.

Use visual media as an alternative to written responses. For example, a teacher assigns students the task of expressing their thinking through visual media, an activity that is effective for eliciting responses from English language learners. However, this same activity also fosters creativity in other students. Students must think out of the box to give a response like this. These types of activities challenge above-grade-level students. They provide opportunities for those artistically gifted students who may struggle academically. And, strategies like this one do not single out English language learners. Strategies like this are what I would call *universal strategies* because they benefit everyone.

Simplify questions to make the language accessible.   Another word for this is *scaffolding*. At times, you will need to rephrase the instructions so your English language learners can understand. This does not mean that you expect less from these students. Simplifying questions has to do with making the language accessible to all students. Higher-order questions can be simplified without cheapening the questions. For example:

- What would happen if . . . ?

- What is your opinion?

- How is _____ related to _____?

- Can you invent _____?

- Would it be better if . . . ?

- Why do you think . . . ?

- If you could _____, what would you do?

- How would you prove . . . ?

- What is the relationship between . . . ?

- What is another way to . . . ?

- Why is this important?

- What ideas justify . . . ?

- What is an original way to show . . . ?

- Why is it better that . . . ?

Provide context to questions to enable understanding. This can be done in the form of pictures or small icons directly next to key words. English language learners also benefit from chunking the sentences. For example, the on-grade-level question might be *How do wind and ocean currents affect the movement of sailboats?* We can add context to this question by chunking the sentence: *In the ocean, wind and ocean currents make boats move. Tell how.* As English language learners read the question, they know right away that the question is about the ocean. Adding context also means providing full names when talking about people. Instead of saying Lincoln, use Abraham Lincoln, President Lincoln, or Mr. Lincoln. Pronouns can be confusing, so use names when possible.

Provide English language learners with sentence stems to encourage higher-order thinking. These learners need the language tools so that they can express what they think. Sentence stems will not only get the information you need and want from your English language learners, but it will also model for them how they should be thinking. You can provide these sentence stems on small sticky notes for students to keep at their desks or write them on laminated cards and distribute them to students when necessary. Here are some sample sentence stems:

- This is important because . . .

- This is better because . . .

- I think _____ because . . .

- I agree with _____ because . . .

- I disagree with _____ because . . .

- I think _____ will happen because . . .

- This is like _____ because . . .

- This is different than _____ because . . .

Partner up, and let partners share aloud. There is confidence in numbers. To progress in the English language, students need to practice speaking the language. This verbal practice can produce anxiety. Just imagine being asked to answer questions in Mandarin in China in a room full of people who have spoken Mandarin from birth. At times, it is appropriate for students to work with partners who are language proficient. These students can work together answering questions, solving problems, or creating projects. Language-proficient partners can provide the academic vocabulary that English language learners need. However, you must prepare your language proficient students to work with language learners by explaining that they must speak slowly and clearly. They also need to be conscious of sharing the work. They need to give these learners time to think and speak. They can remind these learners of the sentence stems, too. Everything must stem from respect.

Engaging students is key to getting them to learn. When teaching reading, teachers need to use engaging relevant literature. Some call this *culturally relevant literature*. However, it does not mean that the teacher must find literature that comes from that country or is about people from that country. Rather, it is finding what students are interested in and capitalizing on it. If students are obsessed with cars, technology, or cell phones, find literature about those topics. Preteach those vocabulary words. Anytime a lesson contains unfamiliar vocabulary, the vocabulary must be taught first so that it can be applied in context. Typically, this activity needs to be done in homogeneous groups rather than with the entire class, especially if the rest of the class already knows the vocabulary. Engage the rest of the class in another activity and then work with English language learners to prepare them for the lesson.

Vary your approaches to reading. Use audio recordings to enhance and model fluent readings. The teacher does not need to fill the entire class time with listening to the audio; just short clips are enough. Even reading aloud can model fluency. Have the class read short pieces in choral readings. By doing this, no one is singled out and everyone gets practice reading aloud in a group.

Take an inquiry approach. It is beneficial for all students to analyze documents or dissect problems for better understanding. One way to do this is to distribute materials and have students analyze, and then explain them. To simplify this process for English language learners, use graphic organizers like KWL charts, Venn diagrams, and T-charts to analyze the patterns and differences they see in the material. If these students cannot write yet, do this as a whole class or small-group activity and use very simple phrases or icons along with key words. Elicit verbal responses from students and then record what they say. Provide them with the academic terms they need to express their thoughts. However, let them take charge in telling what they see and figuring out the important connections.

Make classroom discussions thoughtful ones. During classroom discussions, encourage students to connect their comments with previous comments. This includes saying the name of the person who spoke previously, reviewing what he or she said, giving some sort of opinion based on their comment, and branching out into a new comment. For example, "I agree with Karie when she said the school needs to take a stand on bullying because…." This type of thoughtful discussion encourages students to listen to what others say. It helps them form opinions, which is a higher-order thinking skill. And it helps *all* students, especially English language learners, craft their thoughts into coherent sentences. Be sure to compliment students on how well they discuss. This will go a long way in giving them confidence the next time there is a discussion.

Provide students strong examples when teaching writing. What better examples of writing can we find than in popular literature? For example, how does J.K. Rowling begin *Harry Potter and the Sorcerer's Stone*? We can begin by showing these examples, allowing students to imitate them, and then encouraging students to create their own. Model how to write, but do not do all the work for your students. Elicit examples from students. Do think-alouds, asking how to make it better. Ask for student suggestions and find ways to implement their ideas. Show students how to use a thesaurus. Then, let students practice doing these things. When I teach fiction writing, I choose five diverse fiction books by different authors and then have my students bring their favorite book to class. If you have ever attempted fiction writing (or any writing for that matter), you know that the first lines can be the toughest. I had one rule: My students could not use *Once upon a time* to begin their stories. We examined these pieces of literature as models. I read aloud the beginning lines to the stories I chose. Students shared the opening sentence of their favorite books. We talked about how they were all different. Then I challenged them to modify these and create their own beginning lines. The results were astounding. Another way to provide strong examples is by using word walls. Word walls can be applied in all content-area classes. This can be done by dividing the wall into color codes, separating action verbs, adjectives, nouns, adverbs, etc., and then grouping words by themes or units. These words are examples that can help students produce stronger pieces of writing, whether it is creative writing, reflective writing, or just answering questions. It is important to encourage these learners to use words from the word walls in the classroom.

Open-ended activities allow English language learners to think deeply. These activities have many possible outcomes depending on students' interests, opinions, points of view, and creativity. At times, the teacher will need to tweak the product so that these students can successfully complete the activity. For example, instead of asking for a one-page written response, allow a cartoon strip that tells the same information. Or, allow students to act out their answers. Open-ended activities can be tough to grade, so teachers need to have a good set of rubrics that clarify how the project needs to show student understanding.

Use creative dramatics in all content areas. Allowing English language learners opportunities to act out answers is one way of letting them respond in a nonthreatening way. However, it is good for all students to use creative dramatics. This gives students opportunities to think differently about how to answer a question.

They must create answers non-traditionally, which is a higher-order thinking skill. Examples of this can be tableaux where students work together to create a freeze-frame picture scene with their bodies. Creative dramatics also includes using expression to create meaning. It is acting out and role-playing. All these activities that fall under the heading of creative dramatics are beneficial to English language learners and help encourage creativity in all students.

Conclusion

As much as anyone else, English language learners are capable of using higher-order thinking skills. The problem is that teachers just do not know how to get these learners to think on higher levels. Many of the strategies that can be used to help English language learners think critically and creatively involve some form of making the language accessible to these learners. These strategies include using visual media as alternatives to written responses, simplifying questions, adding context to the language for understanding, providing sentence stems, and partnering students for support. Other strategies are accepted as good teaching practices. These include using engaging literature, varying reading techniques, taking an inquiry approach to learning, holding thoughtful classroom discussions, providing students with strong writing examples, creating open-ended activities, and using creative dramatics in all content areas.

Let's Think and Discuss

1. In what ways has your thinking changed regarding higher-order thinking skills and English language learners?

2. Think about a challenging question you use with your on-grade-level students. What can you do to add context to that question for your English language learners?

3. Think about some lessons coming up. When can you use the sentence stems or question stems in your class?

Chapter 9

Assessing Higher-Order Thinking Skills

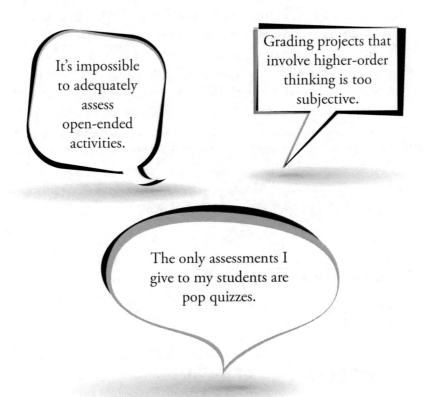

It's impossible to adequately assess open-ended activities.

Grading projects that involve higher-order thinking is too subjective.

The only assessments I give to my students are pop quizzes.

At first glance, it may seem nearly impossible to assess higher-order thinking skills objectively. Some higher-order thinking skills are open-ended, but that does not mean that these skills cannot be assessed. The focus should be on whether students have demonstrated higher-order thinking. Effective assessment always begins with good lesson planning. And furthermore, assessment is something that is not just done at the end of a unit. Assessment should be ongoing throughout units of study.

To begin assessing, teachers need to know what they want to assess. This should be first and foremost with any assignment. One of the best ways to do this is to plan the lesson backwards, or rather plan with the end in mind. Doing this is like thinking of a target. Where do we want to land when this is all said and done? What final results are we looking for? Looking at units of study in this way helps teachers to better think through their desired results of the unit of study. Grant Wiggins and Jay McTighe (1998) have coined the term "enduring understandings" in their book *Understanding by Design*. They ask what enduring understandings students should have as a result of a unit of study. Thinking in this way about lesson planning helps teachers to be in control of what goes on in the classroom with regards to learning and plan lessons that move students toward the desired goal. Wiggins and McTighe (2005) have a three-step process for curriculum design that includes the following:

1. Identifying the desired results

2. Determining the assessment evidence

3. Planning learning experiences

Identifying the Desired Results

Teachers can begin by asking what the goals or objectives they want students to reach are. What do they want their students to learn or be able to do as a result of these lessons? This keeps teachers from making the mistake of just trying to get through a lesson to get through a unit of study, so that they can begin the next unit of study. It gives our teaching a planned purpose instead of a string of disconnected activities. Once the big ideas are determined, the road map is on its way to being designed to get students from where they are to where we want them to be.

Too often, teachers are bogged down with all the content that must be covered within a year. To be most effective, teachers must select the most important things to teach and teach them well.   In her book, *Backwards Planning*, Harriet Isecke (2011) warns against trying to cover too much content.   She says that ". . . covering too much content could lead to the development of disconnected rather than connected knowledge. It might actually prevent students from organizing what they know because they don't have enough time to learn it in sufficient depth" (2011, 21). In essence, depth should take precedence over breadth. Planning with the end in mind takes the most important skills and understandings that need to be taught. Adding in tasks that help develop higher-order thinking skills is a big bonus.   Remember, higher-order thinking skills are something that students might practice in a specific content-area lesson, but students who develop higher-order thinking skills should be able to transfer and apply them in new contexts.

Determining the Assessment Evidence

Assessments should match the learning objectives.   Assessments that only test whether students have memorized facts in isolation do not give those students a deep understanding of the concepts. In these situations, there is little hope that any of the knowledge gained will transfer. Instead, assessments should focus on conceptual understandings. It is also important to remember that when posing a test question that at first glance seems to be based on analysis, it is not higher-order thinking if that same question was used in a classroom discussion. In this situation, the question becomes a basic recall question because students have not had to think this through. Instead, they just had to recall that discussion and summarize it.

The best assessments will point out where students are lacking in their knowledge and application. Then, teachers can take what they have learned from the assessments and make necessary changes to instruction so that students can learn. To make the most of learning, feedback to students is crucial. If assessments are only offered at the end of a unit, the feedback has come too late to make changes in what students think about the topic of study. In these instances, the purpose of the assessment failed in helping students to change their thinking on a topic or to reinforce correct thinking about a topic. Instead, the information that came from the assessment is too late to act upon.

To plan for the best assessments, teachers should ask the following questions:

- How will students show that they have mastered this objective?

- What assessment piece is best for determining whether students have mastered the objective?

Assessments come in a variety of forms and should focus on whether students have demonstrated higher-order thinking. But just how do students demonstrate that they are using higher-order thinking skills? These skills can be demonstrated in many ways, including the following:

- In the questions students ask: Do these questions show that they are thinking about the concepts?

- In the projects students create: Do these projects show something original, a new twist on an old item, or a thoughtful analysis of the topic?

- In the answers students give: Do these answers show that students are not merely restating facts but really taking in the knowledge and making sense of how it connects to other things? Can students explain their thinking?

Many of these assessments can be in the form of verbal checklists. For example, a teacher can make a class checklist that includes a column with student names and columns with the desired outcomes. Teachers can ask questions, perform informal observations, or grade work that demonstrates these outcomes. As each student does this, he or she should receive a check mark in those columns. Checklists can be adapted to any type of study. They help teachers keep track of the level of understanding among students at a quick glance. Teachers can use the information on these checklists to make adjustments so that all students learn and demonstrate higher-order thinking before the end of the unit of study. Questions teachers ask on a checklist can follow the strategies listed in this book on questioning. The following figure is a visual representation of what a checklist may look like.

Fig. 9.1 Example of a Checklist

Student	Can show different points of view on the same topic	Can identify bias	Makes thoughtful arguments to defend answers	Comments
Joanne C.	✓			
Carlos D.	✓	✓		
Marcus F.			✓	
Jordan G.	✓			
Tamika M.	✓			
Jumal P.	✓	✓	✓	Has a strong grasp. Ready for new challenge.
Mary Q.				
John S.	✓	✓		
Petra T.			✓	

Rubrics are also helpful in assessing higher-order thinking. As in all rubrics, specific skills and the degree to which they have been met can be listed as the criteria on the rubric. The criteria should be clear and should assess whether higher-order thinking took place. One good example of this is the criteria normally listed in constructed responses. The following figure is a visual representation of what a rubric may look like:

Fig. 9.2 Example of a Rubric

Student name: <u>Suhad S.</u>	
✓	Demonstrates an understanding of the key concepts.
	Uses solid examples when defending answers.
✓	Draws on relevant information from other examples to support his/her opinions/answers.
✓	Expresses ideas in an original way; does not simply restate answers from the text.
	Is persuasive when defending answers.

When using scoring rubrics, it is usually easier to have three categories: *yes* or *completely*, *somewhat* or *partially*, and *no* or *not at all*. Too many categories can make scoring vague and difficult. Always keep it simple and to the point to get the best results for both your students and you as a teacher. The following figure is a visual representation of what a scoring rubric may look like:

Fig. 9.3 Example of a Scoring Rubric

	Yes, always; Completely	Sometimes; Partially	No, never; Not at all
Student questions show he or she is analyzing			
Student's comments demonstrate creative thinking			
Student forms opinions and defends reasoning			

In recent years, mathematics has taken a turn on many standardized tests. Students must explain their work and not just work out the problem to find the correct answer. This involves a measure of higher-order thinking because students must show their thinking processes. One of the best ways to train students to do this is by teaching them higher-order processes. Once students have enough practice with them, they will be able to use them on their own in new problems. The skills transfer to other concepts and topics. As students learn how to respond in this fashion, their responses should show growth. For example, a teacher will notice that some students are better at explaining their thinking. Students who need to work on this at greater length should receive specific instruction on how to improve their responses.

Other quick ideas for assessment can include the popular ticket-out-the-door strategy. The question or response that students should give on these tickets need to be quick and not lengthy but can still be based on higher-order thinking. And they need to be quick for grading purposes.

Planning Learning Experiences

Once the goals and assessment pieces are identified, then the tasks that can bring about those goals should be planned. What are the best lessons that support both the goals of the unit and the assessment? Teachers will ask how they can get students to reach these objectives. What tasks support these goals? How can we make the big ideas of the unit meaningful to students? What tasks do students need to perform so that they can answer the assessment pieces correctly?

Within this context, teachers will want to employ different strategies that support higher-order thinking. Higher-order thinking strategies support deep connections. They can make learning about a topic meaningful and valuable. Many active strategies supporting higher-order thinking have been outlined in this book and include questioning, problem-solving strategies, decision-making strategies, thinking organizers, project-based learning, open-ended tasks, brainstorming tasks, and creative tasks. Use these when planning your lessons.

To effectively plan the learning experiences, teachers should choose the *best* strategy for the particular lesson. As discussed previously in this book, certain strategies that develop higher-order thinking skills work better in different content areas.

Conclusion

Assessment should be the cornerstone of lesson planning, and should also be ongoing and not something done only at the end of a unit. There are solid ways to design assessments that assess higher-order thinking. Do these questions show that students are thinking about the concepts? Do these projects show something original, a new twist on an old item, or a thoughtful analysis of the topic? Do these answers show that students are not merely restating facts but are really taking in the knowledge and making sense of how it connects to other things? Can students explain their thinking? When planning lessons, teachers should plan backwards. First, they should decide what they want students to learn. Then, an assessment should be created that measures the desired outcome. This can be done in many ways, including rubrics, checklists, and test questions. Even on open-ended activities, good lessons are designed with desired outcomes. Did students exhibit those outcomes? The following lessons should be planned around the assessment.

Let's Think and Discuss

1. What is your approach to planning lessons?

2. Are there some ways you can improve your assessment pieces?

3. What worries you the most about assessment and higher order thinking?

Chapter 10

Putting It All Together

Where do I begin? I feel overwhelmed!

What if I make a mistake?

What if my students refuse to participate?

What do I need to do to be most effective at using higher-order thinking skills?

Designing lessons that encourage higher-order thinking takes planning and thoughtful consideration. Not all strategies mentioned in this book will work the same in every content area. Some are a more natural fit than others.

Selecting a Strategy

It is important to be successful when using new strategies. When designing lessons that build higher-order thinking skills, teachers should not start with the hardest strategy. They can begin with a strategy that seems easy to them or one that they are most interested in trying. They can start with one or two strategies each week, and progressively add more strategies as they feel confident and as the strategy fits with the topic of study. Teachers should not completely write a new lesson. Instead, they can find ways to incorporate these strategies into lessons they have already taught. Know that not everything will work perfectly. If things do not go smoothly, they should not give up. Teachers should continue tweaking and trying the strategy until they understand it thoroughly and see results of higher-order thinking in their students. It is a process. Just as teachers need practice in planning good lessons, students need repetition of strategies to build higher-order thinking skills.

Creating a Plan

Incorporating higher-order thinking into the classroom requires creating a plan. The following steps demonstrate how a teacher can begin with easier strategies and gradually add more complex strategies as he or she feels confident and has more time for planning:

1. Begin with using questioning strategies with your lessons. Bloom's Taxonomy is the best choice because it is teacher-friendly. Start by focusing on the analyzing, evaluating, and creating questions by using the sentence stems.

2. Choose a lesson with a topic that works well for brainstorming. Plan the brainstorm at the beginning of the lesson so that it gets students thinking about the topic. Make the question open-ended so that there could be many answers. Do this brainstorm as a class. (As a replacement, design a thinking organizer for students to record their ideas.)

3. Tie the brainstorm into a lesson on creative writing. Think about how students can write creatively to show what they have learned or studied.

4. Plan a discussion in class, using the Socratic Method. Think about what you want students to gain by the end of the discussion and plan the questions to lead students in that direction. Write the questions based on higher-order thinking skills to guide the discussion.

5. Use a novel, a picture with people, or a primary source to get students to empathize by incorporating creative dramatics. (Perhaps this could lead to a simulation to immerse students in the character, time period, or concept.)

6. Change a lesson to include a product that supports level three or four of Depth of Knowledge.

7. Tackle a more difficult strategy. Create questions based on Williams's Taxonomy or SCAMPER. Teachers should not force any of the levels of these strategies; rather, they should select the ones that fit the best. Ideally, teachers should select four questions that apply to each strategy.

Depending on what grade level and content areas the teacher teaches, each plan will look a little different. It is not easy to plan lessons, and time is always a concern for busy teachers. However, keep in mind that the results will pay off in the end. Seeing the lightbulb go on when a student realizes his or her thoughts have value and that he or she can think for himself or herself is a huge breakthrough. Unfortunately, students are trained to give us the right answer. This type of teaching and learning has hijacked teachers for too long. Teachers need to produce students who have the confidence to think for themselves and who can brainstorm their own ideas and questions. This makes the learning process rich and powerful.

Much of this type of lesson planning is natural, as our kindergarten teachers pointed out. It stems from being a teacher who is a thinker. Take a hard look at how you are living your life. Do you inquire about things? Do you use higher-order thinking on a daily basis? Are you a lifelong learner? Is your life rich and exciting? When you begin living like this, you cannot help but let it spill over into the classroom. Be the teacher who inspires your students to grow. Be the person you need to be.

When teachers know that lessons are built on higher-order thinking, it will add excitement to their teaching and their classroom. Students who have been passive will become active. These lessons will cause them to care and invest themselves, and in the process, they will learn the important content and skills that will enrich their lives.

Assessment

Assessment is always key to good lessons, especially lessons that build higher-order thinking skills. Assessment tells us how students are progressing in their higher-order thinking skills. Do not forget to add in this important element not just at the end of the lesson, but infused throughout your lessons so you can make adjustments where needed. The key is the right amount of challenge to keep your students engaged and learning.

Conclusion

There are many more strategies that promote higher-order thinking. I have covered only a few of them in this book. In everything teachers plan, it is important for them to remember to ask themselves if students are thinking and building those important skills that produce 21st century learners and will benefit by them throughout their lives.

Let's Think and Discuss

1. Where will you begin to implement more higher-order thinking?

2. What kind of support system can you create that will help you to do this?

3. What are some things you can do to promote higher-order thinking skills in the way you live your life?

References Cited

Amis, M. 1991. *Time's arrow*. New York: Crown Publishing Group.

Anderson, L., R. David, and D. Krathwohl, et al. (Eds.) 2001. *A taxonomy for learning, teaching, and assessing: A revision of Bloom's Taxonomy of educational objectives*. Boston, MA: Allyn and Bacon.

Barell, J. 1984. Reflective thinking and education for the gifted. *Roeper Review* 6: 194–196.

———. 1991a. Creating our own pathways: Teaching students to think and become self-directed. In *Handbook of gifted education*, ed. N. Colangelo and G.A. Davis, 256–272. Boston, MA: Allyn & Bacon.

———. 1991b. *Teaching for thoughtfulness*. White Plains, NY: Longman.

———. 2003. *Developing more curious minds*. Alexandria, VA: Association for Supervision and Curriculum Development.

Barron, B. 2008. Powerful learning: Studies show deep understanding derives from collaborative methods. *Edutopia*. http://www.edutopia.org/inquiry-project-learning-research.

Beyer, B. 1987. *Practical strategies for the teaching of thinking*. Boston, MA: Allyn & Bacon.

———. 1988. *Developing a thinking skills program*. Boston, MA: Allyn & Bacon.

Block, C. 1997. *Teaching the language arts: Expanding thinking through student-centered instruction*. Needham, MA: Allyn & Bacon.

Bloom, B., and D. Krathwohl. 1956. *Taxonomy of educational objectives: The classification of educational goals, by a committee of college and university examiners. Handbook i: Cognitive domain.* New York: Longmans, Green.

Bolton, G. 1979. *Toward a theory of drama in education.* London: Longman.

Bransford, J., N. Franks, and R. Sherwood. 1986. New approaches to instruction: Because wisdom can't be taught. Paper presented at the Conference on Similarity and Analogy, University of Illinois, Champaign-Urbana.

Bredekamp, S. 1990. *Developmentally appropriate practice in early childhood programs serving children from birth through age 8* (Expanded Edition). Washington, DC: National Association for the Education of Young Children.

Bredemeier, M., and C. Greenblat. 1981. The educational effectiveness of simulation games: A synthesis of findings. *Simulation & Games 112* (3): 69–73.

Bronson, P., and A. Merryman. 2010. The creativity crisis. *Newsweek,* July 10.

Caine, R., and G. Caine. 1997. *Education on the edge of possibility.* Alexandria, VA: Association for Supervision and Curriculum Development.

Carr, K. 1988. How can we teach critical thinking? *Childhood Education.* 65 (2): 69–73.

Cox, C. 1983. Forum: Informal classroom drama. *Language Arts,* 60: 370–372.

Cummins, J. 1994. Knowledge, power, and identity in teaching English as a second language. In *Educating second language children,* ed. F. Genesee, 33–58. New York: Cambridge Press.

————. 2000. *Language, power and pedagogy: Bilingual children in the crossfire.* Clevedon, England: Multilingual Matters.

Davis, G., and S. Rimm. 1998. *Education of the gifted and talented.* Boston, MA: Allyn & Bacon, Inc.

De Bono, E. 1970. *Lateral thinking: Creativity step by step.* New York: Harper and Row Publishers.

————. 2008. *Creativity workout.* Berkeley, CA: Ulysses Press.

Dewey, J. 1916. *Democracy and Education. An introduction to the philosophy of education.* Repr., New York: Free Press, 1966.

Diamond, M., and J. Hopson. 1998. *Magic trees of the mind: How to nurture your child's intelligence, creativity, and healthy emotions from birth through adolescence.* New York: Dutton.

Dong, Y. 2004. *Teaching language and content to linguistically and culturally diverse students: Principles, ideas, and materials.* Greenwich, CT: Information Age Publishing.

————. 2006. Learning to think in English. *Educational Leadership* 64 (2): 22–26. Alexandria, VA: Association for Supervision and Curriculum Development.

Donohue-Smith, M. 2006. Improving the questions students ask. *The Chronicle of Higher Education* 5 (52).

Edwards, L. 1997. *The creative arts: A process approach for teachers and children.* Upper Saddle River, NJ: Simon and Schuster.

Finkle, S., and L. Torp. 1995. *Introductory documents.* Aurora, IL: Center for Problem-Based Learning.

Froese, V. 1996. *Whole-language: Practice and theory.* Needham, MA: Allyn & Bacon.

Fryer, M. 1996. *Creative teaching and learning.* London: Paul Chapman Publishing.

Gardner, H. 1993. *Multiple intelligences: The theory in practice.* New York: Basic Books.

Geirland, J. 1996. Go with the flow: An interview with Mihaly Csikszentmihalyi. *Wired.* 4 (9): September.

Genesee, F. 1994. Introduction. In *Educating second language children,* ed. F. Genesee, 1–12. New York: Cambridge University Press.

Gibbs, N. 1995. The EQ factor. *TIME Magazine,* October 5.

Gojak, L. 2011. *What's your math problem?!?* Huntington Beach, CA: Shell Education.

Goleman, D. 2006. *Emotional intelligence: 10th anniversary edition: Why it can matter more than IQ.* New York: Bantam Dell.

Harp, B. 1988. When the principal asks: "Is all that drama taking valuable time away from reading?" *The Reading Teacher* 41: 938–940.

Harth, E. 1995. *The creative loop.* Reading, MA: Addison-Wesley.

Heinig, R. 1993. *Creative drama for the classroom teacher,* 4th ed. Englewood Cliffs, NJ: Simon and Schuster.

Henderson, L., and J. Shanker. 1978. The use of interpretive dramatics versus basal reader workbooks. *Reading World* 17: 239–243.

Holt, J. 1983. *How children learn.* New York: Delta.

Honigh, A. S. 2000. Promoting creativity in young children. Paper presented at the Annual Meeting of the Board of Advisors for Scholastic, Inc., New York. (ERIC Document Reproduction Service No. 442548).

Hyde, A. 2006. *Comprehending math*. Portsmouth, NH: Heinemann.

International Society for Technology in Education (ISTE) 2007. NETS for students. http://www.iste.org/standards/nets-for-students-2007.aspx (accessed July 8, 2011).

Isecke, H. 2011. *Backwards planning: Building enduring understanding through instructional design*. Huntington Beach, CA: Shell Education.

Jacobs, B., M. Schall, and A. Scheibel. 1993. A quantitative dendritic analysis of Wernicke's area in humans: Gender, hemispheric, and environmental factors. *Journal of Comparative Neurology* 327 (1): 97–111.

Jacobs, H. 2010. *Curriculum 21: Essential education for a changing world*. Alexandria, VA: Association for Supervision and Curriculum Development.

Jensen, E. 1998. *Teaching with the brain in mind*. Alexandria, VA: Association for Supervision and Curriculum Development.

Johnson, A. 1998. How to use creative dramatics in the classroom. *Childhood Education* 75: (1): 2–6.

Johnson, D., and R. Johnson. 1999. *Learning together and alone: Cooperative, competitive, and individualistic learning*. Boston: Allyn & Bacon. Keene, E., and S. Zimmermann. 1997. *Mosaic of thought: Teaching comprehension in a reader's workshop*. Portsmouth, NH: Heinemann.

Kelner, L. 1993. *The creative classroom: A guide for using creative drama in the classroom, pre K–6.* Portsmouth, NH: Heinemann.

Kotulak, R. 1996. *Inside the brain.* Kansas City, MO.: Andrews and McMeel.

Larmer, J., and J. Mergendoller. 2010. 7 essentials for project-based learning. *Educational Leadership* 68: 34–37.

Leader, W. 1995. *How and why to encourage metacognition in learners.* Paper presented at the meeting of the National Association for Gifted Children, Tampa, FL.

Levin, J. 1981. On the functions of pictures in prose. In *Neuropsychological and cognitive processes in reading,* ed. F. J. Pirozzolo and M. C. Wittrock, 203–228. San Diego: Academic Press.

Lou, Y., P. Abrami, J. Spence, C. Paulsen, B. Chambers, and S. Apollonio. 1996. Within-class grouping: A meta-analysis. *Review of Educational Research* 66 (4): 423–458.

Macceca, S. 2007. *Reading strategies for social studies.* Huntington Beach, CA: Shell Education.

Marzano, R., D. Pickering, and J. Pollock. 2001. *Classroom instruction that works: Research-based strategies for increasing student achievement.* Alexandria, VA: Association for Supervision and Curriculum Development.

Michalko, M. 2006. *Thinkertoys: A handbook of creative-thinking techniques.* Berkeley, CA: Ten Speed Press.

Miller, G., and G. Mason. 1983. Dramatic improvisation: Risk-free role playing for improving reading performance. *The Reading Teacher* 37: 128–131.

National Council of Teachers of Mathematics (NCTM). 2000. *Principles and standards for school mathematics.* Reston, VA: The National Council of Teachers of Mathematics, Inc.

National Research Council (NRC). 1996. National science education standards. Washington, DC: National Academy Press.

Nolan, C. 2000. *Memento.* Hollywood, CA: Summit Entertainment.

Norris, S., and R. Ennis. 1989. *Evaluating critical thinking.* Pacific Grove, CA: Critical Thinking Press and Software.

National Science Education Standards (NSES). 1996. Washington, D.C.: The National Academies Press.

Osborn, A. 1993. *Applied imagination: Principles and procedures of creative problem-solving, 3rd edition.* Amherst, MA: Creative Education Foundation.

Partnership for 21st Century Skills. 2004. Framework for 21st century learning. http://www.p21.org/index.php?option-com=content&task=view&id=254&ltemid=120 (accessed July 8, 2008).

Paul, R., and L. Elder. 2002. *Critical thinking: Tools for taking charge of your professional and personal life.* Upper Saddle River, NJ: Pearson Education, Inc.

Petranek, C. 1994. A maturation in experiential learning: Principles of simulation and gaming. *Simulation & Gaming* 25: 513–523.

Piaget, J. 1969. *The psychology of the child.* New York: Basic Books.

Pogrow, S. 2005. HOTS revisited: A thinking development approach to reducing the learning gap after grade 3. *Phi Delta Kappan* 87: 64–75.

Raiffa, H. 1968. *Decision analysis: Introductory lectures on choices under uncertainty*. Upper Saddle River, NJ: Addison-Wesley.

Randel, J., B. Morris, C. Wetzel, and B. Whitehill. 1992. The effectiveness of games for educational purposes: A review of the research. *Simulation & Gaming* 25: 261–276.

Rhem, J. 1998. Problem-based learning: An introduction. *The National Teaching & Learning Forum* 9 (1).

Rowland-Dunn, J. 1989. Making time for critical thinking skills. *Instructor* 99 (2): 36–37.

Salovey, P., and J. Mayer. 1990. Emotional intelligence. *Imagination, Cognition, and Personality 9*: 185–211.

Sautter, R. 1994. An arts education school reform strategy. *Phi Delta Kappan* 74: 432–437.

Scriven, M., and R. Paul. 1987. *Defining critical thinking*. Dillion Beach, CA: National Council for Excellence in Critical Thinking Instruction. http://www.criticalthinking.org/pageID=766&categoryID=51 (accessed September 15, 2010).

Smith, C. 1990. Two approaches to critical thinking. *Reading Teacher* 44 (4): 350–351.

Strom, R. 2000. Parents and grandparents as teachers. In *On the Edge and Keeping on the Edge*, ed. E.P. Torrance, 53–76. Westport, CT: Ablex Publishing.

Strong, R., H. Silver, and M. Perini. 2001. *Teaching what matters most: Standards and strategies for raising student achievement*. Alexandria, VA: Association for Supervision and Curriculum Development.

Thibault, M., and D. Walbert. 2010. *Reading images: an introduction to visual literacy.* http://www.learnnc.org/lp/pages/675 (accessed November 15, 2010).

Treffinger, D., S. Isaken, and B. Stead-Dorval. 2006. *Creative problem solving: An introduction.* Waco, TX: Prufrock Press.

Tyler, R. 1949. *Basic principles of curriculum and instruction.* Chicago: University of Chicago Press.

Van Sickle, R. 1986. A quantitative review of research on instructional simulation gaming: A twenty-year perspective. *Theory and Research in Social Education* 14 (3): 245–264.

Von Winterfeldt, D., and W. Edwards. 1986. *Decision analysis and behavioral research.* New York: Cambridge University Press.

Wagner, B. 1988. Research currents: Does classroom drama affect the arts of language? *Language Arts* 65: 46–55.

Wallas, G. 1926. *The art of thought.* New York: Hartcourt.

Wiggins, G., and J. McTighe. 1998. *Understanding by design.* Alexandria, VA: Association for Supervision and Curriculum Development.

———. 2005. *Understanding by design: Expanded 2nd edition.* Alexandria, VA: Association for Supervision and Curriculum Development.

Wineburg, S., and J. Schneider. 2009. Inverting Bloom's Taxonomy. Education Week, October. http://www.edweek.org/ew/articles/2009/10/07/06wineburg.h29.html (accessed October 2, 2009).

Wolf, S. 1993. What's in a name? Labels and literacy in readers theater. *The Reading Teacher* 46: 540–545.